A CASTERBRIDGE IRONMONGER
THURMANS OF DORCHESTER
1863 - 1966

J. E. SKYRME

Edited by his daughter
ELIZABETH ROWBOTHAM
Illustrated by
Jane Comben and Jill Smith

E.M. Rowbotham
Dell Cottage, Plaisters Lane,
Sutton Poyntz, Weymouth,
Dorset DT3 6LQ

©Copyright Elizabeth Rowbotham 1993.

Typeset by M.E. King, St Andrews Road, Bridport, Dorset
Printed by Sherrens the Printers
Units 1 and 2, South Park, Avon Close,
Granby Industrial Estate, Weymouth DT4 9YX

British Library Cataloguing in Publication Data

A CIP record for this book is available
from the British Library

ISBN 0 9522502 0 9

Dedicated to my father, who died in 1981.
This book is a compilation of events recorded by him,
throughout a lifetime associated with the ironmongery trade

Acknowledgments

I should like to thank Topsy Levan for deciphering my Father's handwriting, Jill Smith and Jane Comben for their illustrations, and Anne Bartlett for all the typing.

I should also like to thank the Staff of Thurmans, because without them, this story could not have been written.

E.M.R.

THURMANS OF DORCHESTER

1863 The story starts with an announcement dated 1863 by Mr. M. J. Thurman of Weymouth stating that he was setting up an ironmonger's shop in School Street, Weymouth.

1884 Mr. W.H.C. Thurman, son of M.J. Thurman established an entirely separate ironmongery business at 17 South Street, Dorchester in premises that had been a dwelling-house and is thought to have also at times been a school and the post office.

1898 Mr. W.H.C. Thurman died and the business was purchased by Mr. W.R. Skyrme, possession being taken in September that year.

1905 The business demanded more room, all living accommodation on first and second floors was converted into stores and showrooms and the side entrance from South Street to the dwelling part together with the passage was thrown into the shop.

1911 In the meantime Thurman's workshops (originally the stables) fronting Charles Street were left alone, but in 1911 the whole of the large garden between the front shop and workshops was roofed in, making a continuous roofed building from one street to the other. The original stables now used as workshops were not altered.

1921 Mr. Hughes, ironmonger, of 64 High West Street, Dorchester, died and the premises were bought by Mr. W.R. Skyrme and staffed and stocked as a branch shop.

1924 The front portion of 64 High West Street was reconstructed, a new shop-front fitted and the one side door (East Side) and passageway thrown into the shop.

1926 Mr. W.R. Skyrme died and was succeeded by his son, Mr. J.E. Skyrme.

1930 The workshops were removed from Charles Street to the old stables and coach house at the rear of the High West Street shop fronting Colliton Street (Pease Lane) and the old Charles Street workshops converted into additional stores. At the same time the Old Rectory, inhabited at one time by Rev. John White, in Colliton Street was found to be in an unsafe condition, was made secure and used as stores and garage. This necessitated the removal of the stone arched doorway which was taken intact and built into the south wall of the South Street shop to preserve it.

1931 The 17 South Street premises had reached the limit of its capacity and the entire building except part of the old stores at rear (fronting Charles Street) was demolished and a modern reinforced concrete building was erected on site, being completed in 1932, the business being carried on successfully during the nine months of demolition and reconstruction.

1937 The workshops at rear of 64 High West Street were inadequate and part of the garden was built over and workshops erected, the old buildings being converted into rough stores.

1942 The front portion of 64 High West Street was requisitioned by the Ministry of Food and used as a 'British Restaurant,' the centre and rear including workshops being retained and used by Thurmans.

1946 In accordance with modern practice the business was converted into a private limited company, the directors and only shareholders being Mr. J.E. Skyrme and his brother-in-law Mr. O. Bley.

1950 The 64 High West Street premises were derequisitioned by the Ministry and that portion let to Mr. A.M. Willats for use as an antique furniture shop. On the retirement of Mr. O. Bley (due to ill health) Mr. J.W. Dibben who sold his ironmongery business in South Street adjacent to Agra Place and had joined Thurmans staff in 1938 was appointed co-director.

1957 Mr. Willat's lease having terminated, the High West Street shop again turned over to ironmongery as a 'Farm, Dairy and Garden' branch of the main business.

1963 The site and building of 17 South Street was sold to Messrs. Allied Supplies Ltd., proprietors of Home and Colonial Ltd. who demolished the frontage and the rear stores and turned it into a grocery supermarket.

The 64 High West Street premises had meanwhile been very extensively altered internally to accommodate all the various departments previously carried by the two shops.

1966 64 High West Street was sold to Messrs. Rogers and Dawes Ltd.

1979 Thurmans closed, the premises having been sold to the Cheltenham and Gloucester Building Society.

1980 The Building Society opened its offices at 64 High West Street, having sold the back portion to the Museum. This area, including the old workshops, now houses the Colliton Antique Centre.

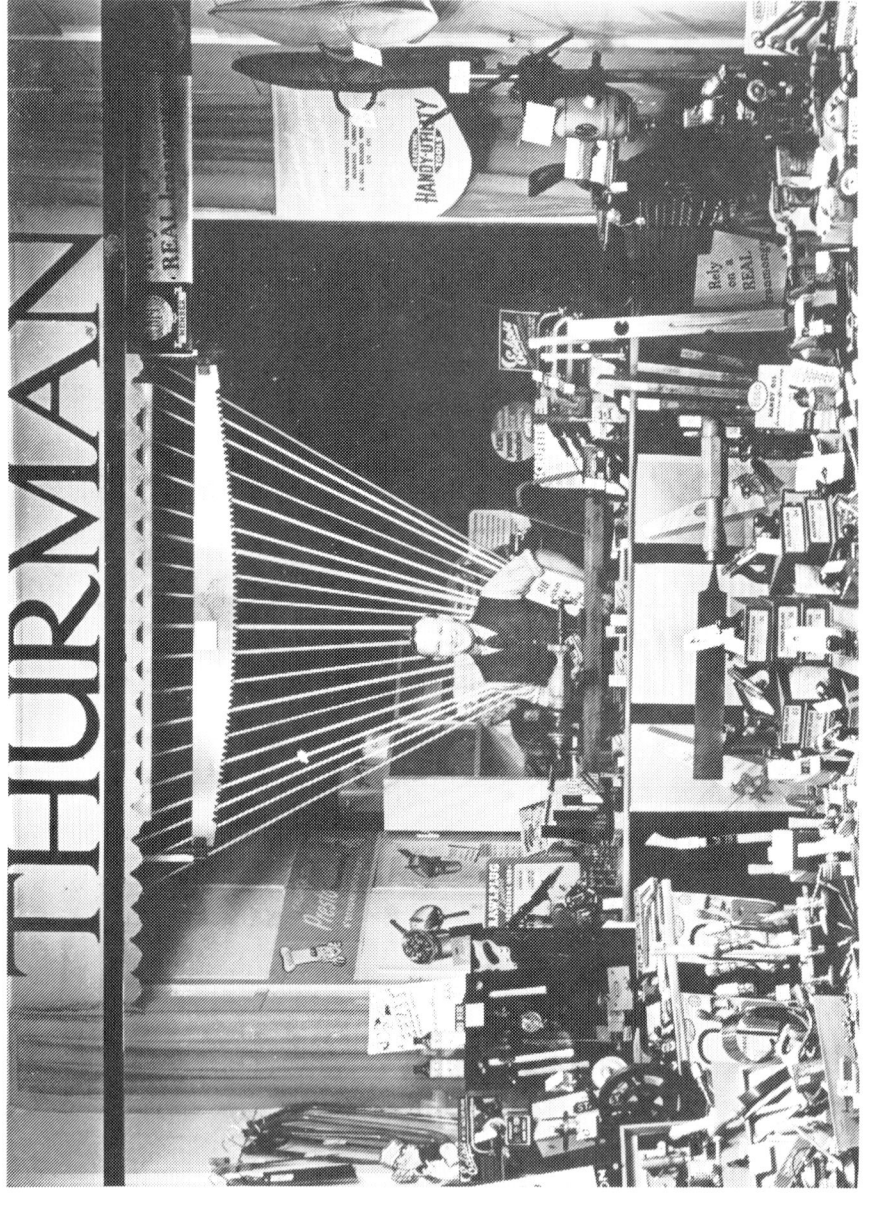

South Street Shop Window Display

Chapter 1 1863 - 1918

During the last half of the nineteenth century, September 1863 to be exact, an ironmongers shop in St. Thomas Street, Weymouth was opened by Mr. M.H. Thurman. His son Mr. William Henry Clayton Thurman was trained as an ironmonger but having disagreed with the family decided to branch out on his own and commence in business in Dorchester. No contact between the two businesses was made and it must be remembered that there were no motor-cars and all contact between the two towns had to be by horse or train.

The date was 1884 and the site chosen was 17 South Street. As it turned out many years afterwards, it was a happy choice, as the new post office was built exactly opposite, and was naturally a focal point for prospective customers.

The premises consisted of a large brick-built house of no particular merit with the ground floor converted into a shop with two windows facing the street and a side door and passage giving access to the living part of the house above.

Behind the building was a large garden with apple and pear trees and a greenhouse. Behind that again, stables, and a coach-house fronting Charles Street. The premises thus had direct access to two streets.

Mr Thurman

Mr Thurman always wore a frock coat and top hat in business and as the custom of those days was to hang all available stock, buckets kettles, frypans, coal scuttles etc. on the ceiling, his movements were patent to all as the hat did battle with the stock-in-trade.

Mr. Thurman was a man of fixed ideas, one of them being that the best orders were to be obtained at the various hostelries, THE ANTELOPE, JUNCTION, KINGS ARMS, PLUME OF FEATHERS etc. on market days which were Wednesdays and Saturdays. He was quite right, but much to the fury of the staff the top-hatted figure invariably tottered back again at the end of the day, dripping pencilled slips of paper from each pocket with instructions that these orders had to 'go out today', the carriers and farmers having all gone home a couple of hours ago.

The staff consisted of Mr. G.W. Watts the manager, Harry King the porter and packer, two junior assistants and an errand boy.

A portion of the stables was converted into a small workshop with forge, the horse and gig formerly housed there were disposed of and the delivery service was confined to a pair of hand-trucks. This was adequate for delivery around the town and especially to the carriers' vans on market days.

All manner of repairs to household utensils and implements were undertaken and the hay loft above the stable was used as a sheet-metal and tinsmith's shop. The workmen were one smith, one fitter, one sheet-metal worker and two juniors. To do work away from the workshop they walked, carrying tools and fittings. If large items had to be moved a horse and cart was hired.

Walking to the nearer villages to carry out a day's work was by no means uncommon and to walk four miles to Moreton, and home again in the evening, carrying a bag of tools was considered part of the job. It was reasoned with some logic that they might as well be paid for walking, as for staying at the bench in the workshop.

The Gas Works in Icen Way was already in being. It distilled the gas into gasometers and main piping but the work of household installation was left to individual plumbers. Thus the business was described as 'Dorset General Hardware Stores, Bell Hangers and Gas Fitters', the bells being the type that were hung in a row in passage or servants' quarters and actuated by cranks and levers. Gas fitting was dropped about 1912.

The country carriers were not only the carriers of goods and small livestock, chickens and an occasional calf, not to mention their suffering passengers, but also served as the shopping service for their district. They would appear at the shop on market days after having parked their covered vans in their appointed places in High East Street, High West Street or various hotel yards, and attended to the needs of their horses, with long lists of their customers' requirements, selecting the type of goods that would suit. 'Mrs. Legg would be happy with a new wash-board of a certain size.' 'Mrs. Foot says she wants a four-gallon oval pot, but I'm going to take her a six-gallon one because they're nine in family and she'll need it.' 'Mr. Dufall wants a pair of string harness traces and a pair of half-cased hames but I'd better look through the traces, his old mare is getting on a bit and needs a light set.' And so it went on through the day.

Mrs. Bale of Crossways recounted the other day a story of her young days helping her father, Mr. Hansford the Moreton carrier.

An old lady living in West Stafford never came to town, but indulged in a new hat each Spring, entrusting the choice to Miss Hansford, who says the choice never failed to give delight. Mrs Bale also remembers, with some reason, an occasion when a crate on the tailboard of the van burst open on the Redbridge road, releasing some half-dozen piglets. It took an hour and the efforts of all the passengers to round them up, and the poor old mare had to gallop all the way to Dorchester to make up time.

Mr. Record of Sydling was known as the 'Midnight Carrier' owing to his late

circa 1910
- Case — Moore Jnr. — Young   W. Dean
(Fitter) (Tinsmith) (Apprentice) (Blacksmith) (Apprentice)

1913
F. Mills   A. Gill   H.G. New   - Moore
Snr.   W. Dean
(Tinsmith) (Apprentice Fitters)

1960
A. Gill   H.G. New
47 years later!

17 South Street 1925
H.Harvey H. King A.J.Ellery Miss E. Stone J. Purceglove L.F. Turner (and office cat)

1955 En route to 'British Industries Fair, Birmingham
H.J. Fry   E.A. Wheadon
(Buyer)   (Workshop Manager)

1955 Going to Stroud about an agency for oil-fired boilers
F.W. Gillett   W.G. Skyrme   J.W. Dibben

1957 Going to Bath and West Agricultural Show, Swindon
T. Laing Miss E.M. Skyrme R. Johns

departure from Dorchester and subsequent delivery of parcels to his outlying customers at any time up to 1 a.m.

Country carriers converging on Dorchester, at one time, numbered 39.

The carriers were the life-blood veins of the villagers and the later intrusion of the impersonal bus services was bitterly resented.

Dorchester seemed to be composed of colourful characters in those days and Mr. W.H.C. Thurman was no exception. His death in 1898 was a loss to the community.

On the death of Mr. W.H.C. Thurman the business was to be sold. It was bought by Mr. William Robert Skyrme and all the staff retained.

Competition in Dorchester was severe. The largest and most efficient ironmongers shop was Hazel and Co., trading in High West Street, once Braggs sports shop. There was also Hughes with very extensive premises at 64 High West Street, next to Holy Trinity Church, and Dibben Bros. in South Street whose shop was next to Agra Place where Shooters Milk Bar[1] once stood. There were also other small shops selling paraffin and sundries and in the side streets several repair shops.

In spite of the change of ownership the original name of Thurmans was retained, as was the custom in an agricultural environment, and the first few years were devoted to consolidating the position.

The first expansion happened in 1905 when the dwelling accommodation was taken into the shop, the upstairs rooms being used as showrooms, one room being used for the storage and display of all kinds of brushware, another for kitchen requisites mostly tinware and wooden articles, knife-polishing machines etc., another room for the then popular japanned goods, hearth furniture, fenders and travelling trunks, yet another room devoted to paraffin lamps and their accessories and the rest as general storerooms of all sorts and sizes.

At the same time the separate passage leading to the house portion was taken into the shop and the ground floor display windows extended to the full width of the building.

The alterations were carried out by Messrs. Watts Bros. of Pound Lane, Fordington (no relation to the Mr. G.W. Watts the manager of Thurmans) under the direction of Mr. F.T. Maltby, architect of Dunloe House, Fordington.

The shop began to be noticed, and attracted the attention of many of the large country houses in the surrounding district.

During this period Harry King was taken from the dispatch room (except market days) and put in charge of a new departure, glass-cutting and fret-wood. Fretwork was a universal home hobby, so fret-wood one-eighth of an inch thick was stocked in oak, walnut, mahogany, satin walnut and cedar in large sheets and cut to customer's required sizes. Paints were not yet available ready-mixed in tins

---

[1] now an Oxfam shop

but were ground on a slab with a mullard using the various ochres, earths and colourings to match customer's tastes. This job was turned over to King. The tradesmen, wheelwrights, carpenters etc. bought the colourings and mixed their own paints.

In addition, cartridge-making was commended. The cases, caps, wads, powder and shot were bought from Eley's and assembled by King using various presses. The shot varied in size from no. 4 for pigeon shooting to no. 8 for game, no. 5 being the general purpose farmers' size. Cartridges under the name of 'Sure Death' put up in boxes of 25 and 100 became very popular and after a while King had to be detailed for that work only.

About this time Mr. Hazel died and his business was bought by two partners, Mr. Whaley and Mr. Windows who changed the trading name of Hazel and Co. to their own, retaining Mr. Venton as an outside representative. Mr. Venton's two sons and a grandson traded as ironmongers in Princes Street[1].

In 1911 the garden of Thurmans was roofed-in with corrugated iron forming a vast storeroom, the largest single span roof in Dorchester at that time. The workshop was enlarged, a Campbell town gas engine installed, power machinery, a lathe, drill, grindstones and lawnmower grinder were bought and put to full use.

Tin kettle

The interest of Mr. G.W. Watts although spread over the business as a whole was very much centred in workshop matters and at his instigation the manufacture of the then popular garden seats and chairs was started. Wrought-iron ends in scrollwork with wooden slats for seat and back rests, and painted green, most uncomfortable but fashionable and ready sellers.

Flue rakes, firing shovels and pokers were made in the smith's shop and the tinsmith's and coppersmith's section manufactured such things as the very popular quick-boiling conical tin kettle, 8" diameter at bottom decreasing to 3.5" at the top, presenting a large heating surface to the flame of fire or gas. These were made

---
[1] Next to Argos

Watering Can

Seed Lip

up in batches of six dozen at a time.

Another very popular article was a milking pail in 3 gallon, 4 gallon and 5 gallon sizes with a very comfortable swaged iron bail handle. These buckets continued to be demanded up to the middle 1950's. The retinning of copper kitchen utensils from the nearer large country houses brought other custom from this very desirable source. Galvanized watering cans, seed lips and coal scuttles were also manufactured. All these articles and many more including cheese vats, cream pans, skimmers etc. were sold by the retail shop.

Hours worked at that time were: Front retail shop 8 a.m. to 7.30 p.m. and to 9 p.m. on Saturdays, Thursdays being the innovation of a half-holiday. Workshop 6 a.m. to 6 p.m. with half-day on Saturdays.

In this period 1908 the Bath and West of England Agricultural Show was held in Dorchester. Thurmans took space and showed for that time, a very comprehensive display of dairy goods, household items including several new inventions including a rotary knife cleaner, Gillette safety razor, and an early type of Daisy vacuum cleaner, also a large selection of farming requisites and tools, sheep-shearers, 12-bore sporting guns, etc. The show was a success.

The Artillery Barracks in Poundbury Road were fully occupied by mounted troops. It so happened that a regular soldier, H.A. Harvey of the Chestnut Troop, Royal Horse Artillery completed his 21 years' service in 1904 while stationed at Dorchester and was discharged with the rank of Bombardier, and a small gratuity. With a wife and two children the gratuity was soon gone and Harvey had to get a job at a time when jobs were hard to find. He applied to Thurmans and was engaged on the lowest rung of the ladder, as a porter.

It was soon noticed that his handwriting was superior to the average, that the dispatch room had assumed a tidier and more methodical appearance and that he had a gift for getting along with customers to whom he delivered parcels. Questioning brought out the fact that during periods of foreign service he had learned languages and could write and converse in French, Italian, Spanish and knew a little Hindustani. Here was good human material indeed, but at that time there was a prejudice against admitting anyone to 'the trade' unless a five years bound apprenticeship had been endured. Accordingly Harvey was promoted, as a first step, from his porterage to the office, and was a success. After a while he was introduced into the front shop and by this time the staff were used to, and accepted him. He quickly developed a flair for display and was put in charge of the main display window, the contents of which were changed every Monday, and which came to be regarded by the locals as one of the sights of Dorchester.

After a while his displays were entered in local competitions, then area contests and finally National promotions. He gained first prize in four National contests and an unrecorded number of first and placings in others.

As a 'National' carried a first of fifty to sixty pounds, a not inconsiderable sum in those days, to be distributed between Harvey and his helpers, his popularity increased somewhat. One of his winning windows was National Aluminium

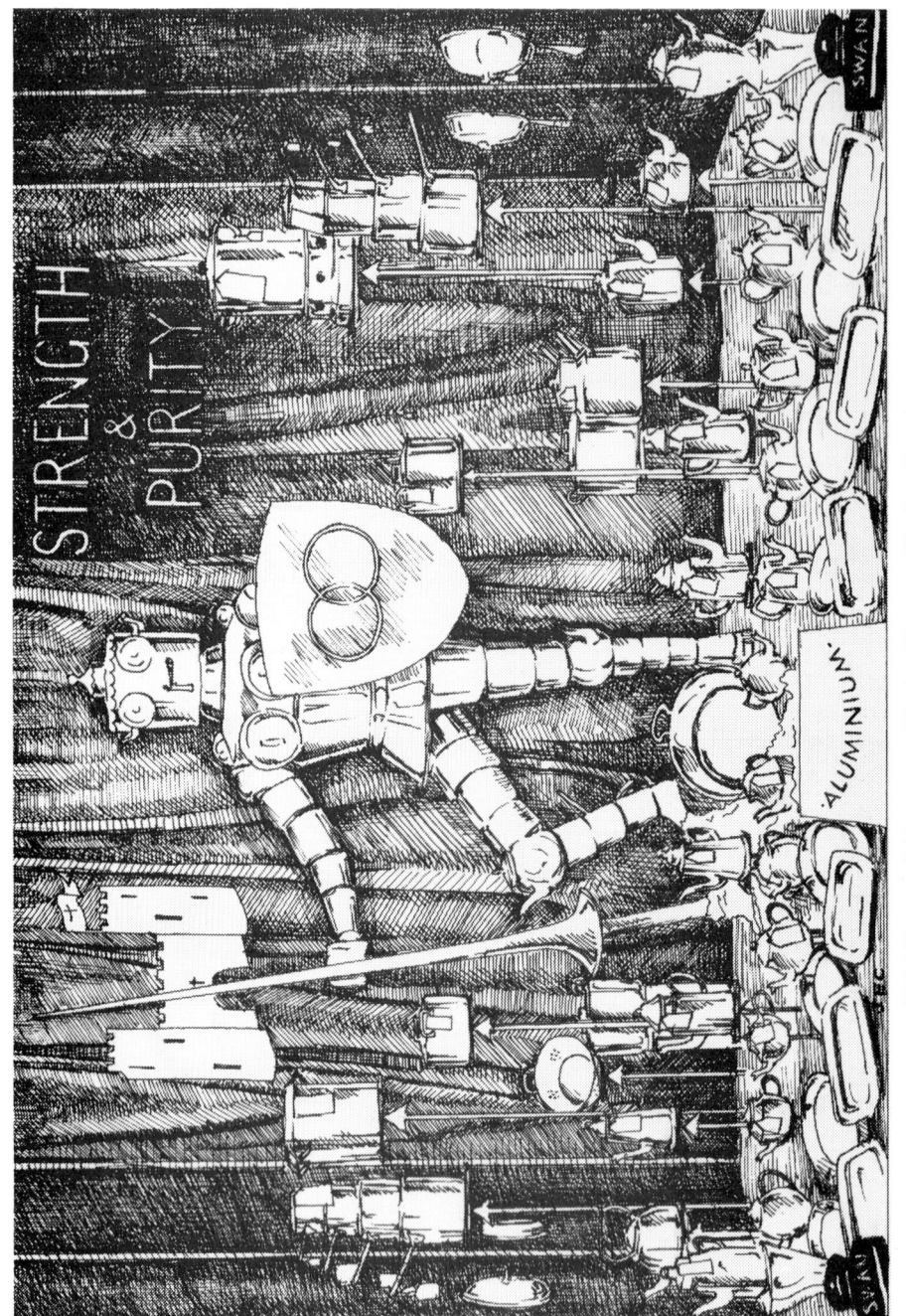

1936 National Aluminium Week - Winning Window Display

Week, promoted jointly by the manufacturers of aluminium household and dairy utensils. Harvey's centrepiece was a full-sized Knight in Armour, made up entirely of aluminium utensils, teapots, buckets, collanders, saucepans, etc. This was publicised in America and many letters were received from the U.S.A., Argentine and other places.

Harvey turned out to be a first-rate salesman, gaining the confidence of the customers. Most of the larger Dorset houses employed butlers and cooks, either French or Italian, who delighted in coming in for a chat in their own language, with a consequent increase of business from those sources.

Thurmans was blessed with a lively lot of apprentices. 'Blessed' is the right word as a vigorous and intelligent apprentice will usually make a first-class workman later on. Their ringleader in pre-1914 days was a workshop apprentice fitter names W. Dean (Bill).

The blacksmith at that time was a man called Young. A good and competent smith, but a surly and unpopular character. One day Dean delivered a message that Young was urgently wanted in the office. Young put the bar-iron he was going to heat on the anvil, and went. On his return, furious at having been caught on a fool's errand, he picked up the iron, yelled and dropped it. In the meantime Bill Dean had heated the iron to blue heat and replaced it exactly where the smith had left it. Having nimble legs, Dean reached Charles Street first and escaped near murder.

When at the anvil Young always stood in the same position bent over his work. Taking careful measurements the lads bored two holes in the tinsmith's shop floor above, one immediately above, and the other a peephole near it. A tin funnel was placed in the hole and a quart jug of cold water placed beside. When Young was seen to be in the right position the water was poured and cascaded down the sweating smith's neck. As there was only one staircase and Young, hammer in hand, was soon halfway up it, there was no escape. It took two fitters to restrain Young and allow the delinquents to get away.

Another trick played on the poor man was to smear the lavatory seat with transparent varnish when it was known that he was to be the next visitor.

The smith was not the only sufferer from the apprentices' high spirits. When the upper part of the house was still occupied, i.e. before the first alterations, the

resident maid's habit was to smuggle a few titbits out to the boys in mid-morning. For some reason or other she upset them and the following morning emerged from the coal-house smothered with a black sticky substance and purple with rage. Her enemies had tarred the top layer of coal. That event cost the family a new apron, starched dress, mob-cap and a week's spoiled and half-cold meals.

It was also noted that the number of times the long workshop ladder had to be carried through the garden for some small repair at the front increased considerably when apples and pears were nearing maturity.

These escapades were of course winked-at and thoroughly enjoyed by the management but relief was felt when the chief butt of the revelries, the smith Young, decided to leave.

Dean joined the Dorset Regiment in August 1914, at the outbreak of war, together with many other spirited young men of Dorchester, was selected for service as a mechanic in the Royal Flying Corps, was attached to General Townsend's Column in the Middle East Campaign, was captured by the Turks at the fall of Kut and died at Kenia in their hands in 1916.

The outbreak of war, August 4th 1914, brought many problems. There was a surge of patriotism and the younger staff felt that they must answer Kitchener's call, and went off to war. The retail side of the business could manage by dint of everyone putting in more time and leaving out non-essentials, also three seniors were either over military age, or could not pass the medical tests. But the workshop was denuded, just at a time when people had to 'make do and mend' instead of discarding and buying new. In October a blacksmith named F. Gillet (Fred) from Somerton, Somerset, rejected by the army because of the loss of a thumb, applied for a job. He proved an excellent smith and general repairer, but one side of his character was not at the time suspected. He was ambitious. It was presently discovered that he was taking, privately, postal courses in electrical engineering, hot-water heating and hydraulics, and that he had gained diplomas. Although these efforts could not be utilized to any degree in wartime, we shall see later that they were to be invaluable. Another side to his character quickly emerged, a quick temper. It is not recorded how many times he gave notice, or was sacked, but as he always turned up the next morning as usual, all was well.

Of the war period there is little to record. It was a question of keeping going, of improvisation, of obtaining any supplies that could be located and trying to help customers to keep their farms and households running. It was also a question of portioning out goods as they came in, to those known to be in most need of them. In the absence of full-scale rationing schemes, the retailer had to be as fair as possible to all. There was of course no wireless broadcasting or T.V. and arrival of daily newspapers tended to be erratic. A small but appreciated service that Thurmans instigated was the setting-up of a desk in the shop bearing a copy of the day's TIMES and any bits of later information that happened to come through, especially war news of any local residents.

One incident illustrating the times may be quoted. In late August 1914 there was an urgent message from the Colonel in charge of an emergency camp set up on the bare heathland at Bovington for a battalion of Kitchener's army recruits. They had tents, bedding, cooking apparatus, food by the ton, in fact everything but cutlery. Apart from pocket-knives brought by some of the men there was not a knife, fork or spoon in the camp. Could Thurmans help? All stocks of cutlery were turned out, staff sent around the other ironmongers to get what was available, a horse and gig hired form Joe Whitty's stables and by 3 p.m. Harvey and a helper set off for Bovington to be greeted by a horde of hungry recruits who accounted for the load before the Commandant's tent could be reached. About a fortnight later the proper Army issue turned up.

That tented camp with its mass of very raw recruits is now the Headquarters of the Royal Armoured Corps; to the locals still known as the 'Tank Camp.'

The war dragged on. The sad list mounted on the TIMES desk, of local lads killed, missing or wounded grew longer, leavened by news of decorations being won. Colliton Park was filled with marquees forming a large military hospital staffed by small cadre of army doctors and nurses, the rest of the staff being local ladies who after a short course of First Aid did their best. The patients were from the Army, Navy and Royal Flying Corps with a large section of Belgian and French. Every day there was the sound of a band playing the Dead March, and a little pathetic procession passing down Cornwall Road to the cemetery. The majority of the large country houses took in as many of the lightly-wounded and convalescent as they could. There was a wonderful spirit running through every section of the community, perhaps never equalled before or since.

The Artillery Barracks, Poundbury Road was used as a prisoner-of-war prison, if indeed it could be called a prison. A little barbed-wire was mounted on the outside walls (on brackets made by Thurmans), working parties strolled down the main streets on their way to the nearer farms, some to Edisons Steam Plough Works[1] and some to Channons in High East Street where they machined shellcases and fuses for the British Army. These parties were 'escorted' by armed troops composed of soldiers medically unfit for service overseas, who had great difficulty in keeping up with, and sometimes in sight of, their prisoners. The rest were taken on route marches for exercise and very decently halted at intervals to allow the guards to catch up.

[1] Now Telecom Depot

'It was rumoured that the rations served to the prisoners were much superior to those for the civilians outside. At any rate the Germans were friendly, every ready to swap tunic-buttons and badges for little luxuries, biscuits etc., and seemed very content to be where they were instead of in the trenches.

Eventually, November 1918, it was all over. Rejoicings and celebrations there were in plenty, tinged with memories of those who could never return. Thurmans stocks of essentials were by now practically non-existent, but war surplus goods quickly came on the market and much could be adapted for use, especially on the farms: lanterns, oil stoves, water pumps, tea cans, crude kitchenware etc., examples of which may be seen in Dorset County Museum. This helped to keep things going until proper supplies began to drift in.

Garden Roller

Chapter 2 1919 - 1929

Most of the pre-war staff came back when released by the Services and in 1920 John Edward Skyrme, the son of the proprietor returned to the business after a brief spell on a farm learning something of the practical side of farming. Agricultural Colleges were in the far distant future. A further period was devoted to attendances at factories in Birmingham, Wolverhampton, Sheffield etc., to gain knowledge as to how the merchandise was actually made.

In 1921 Mr. Robert Hughes, ironmonger, of 64 High West Street, Dorchester[1] died and the premises were bought by Mr. W.R. Skyrme of Thurmans to be used as a branch shop selling general ironmongery with special emphasis on agricultural requirements.

The premises were large: a retail shop on the ground floor with a large Georgian house over. Entrance to the house was by a side door and passage, one side of which was formed by the wall of Holy Trinity Church. The shop had one large display window and entrance was by a series of steps surmounted by a door on the east side of the building. Behind the shop was a garden and a racked store for the storage of iron pipe and bar iron, the sale of which to the country blacksmiths was considerable. Behind that was a sizeable yard with stable and coach-house and beyond that the fabric of the Rectory occupied from 1606 to 1648 by Rev. John White, rector of St. Peter's and Holy Trinity Churches, chiefly remembered for inspiring a group of parishioners to go to America and colonize Massachusetts. The Rectory backed on to Colliton Street, formerly known as Pease Lane, and beside it was a wide entrance from the yard to street. The property thus had access to both High West Street and Colliton Street.

Above the iron store was a 51-feet-long showroom and above that again, storerooms. Cellars devoted to bulk supplies of nails of all descriptions, farm harness chains etc., ran under the whole of the front shop. Perhaps the most valuable display space was a wide strip of private pavement outside the High West Street frontage on which could be displayed all manner of goods in season. No-one using High West Street could possibly fail to see them. The house property was occupied by Mr. G.W. Watts and his two daughters, his wife having died some while previously.

The shop was restocked with general ironmongery, farm equipment and bulky goods such as washing-machines which took up too much space at the South Street shop. A special feature was made of gardening supplies. J.E. Skyrme was placed in charge with W. Hopkins, a Barnstaple man and H.C. Hancock from Newton Abbot, H. Reeves a Dorchester lad and Harry Trevett, an ex-naval Chief

---

[1] Now Cheltenham and Gloucester Building Society

Petty Officer as general handyman. The stables were used as garages and the old Rectory continued in the use as a paraffin and general store.

Although there were now two separate establishments they worked as one unit, stock and staff were interchangeable according to needs, and although there was a certain amount of friendly rivalry as regards sales, all worked together in complete harmony. The fact that practically all were recruited either locally or from Devon and Cornwall may have had something to do with this.

The property had had a long history of ironmongery. It is known to have been owned by 'William Davis and Rebecca his wife,' ironmonger, of Dorchester in 1808 and by Richard Wallis, thought to have been an ironmonger before him.

In 1850 it passed to John Galpin and in 1875 to 'George Crocker the younger' and 'Charles Fenner' who described themselves as 'Ironmonger, Ironfounders, Machinists and Engineers'. In 1879 Charles Fenner dropped out and George Crocker the Younger took Joseph Foster as partner and traded under the name of 'Crocker and Co.' In 1890 Crocker and Foster took John Green Lott into partnership. It seems that it was Crocker who paved the forecourt at his own expense and claimed the right to display goods on it. In 1896 Crocker dropped out and the business continued under the title of 'Foster Lott & Co.' It was probably during the 1890 partnership that the foundry in London Road, Dorchester, later known as 'Lott and Walne' was run in conjunction with the ironmongery business. In 1899 Lott left the partnership and J. Foster sold 64 High West Street and the business to Robert Hughes who has been mentioned before. J.G. Lott retained his interest in the foundry, taking J.J. Walne into partnership. On J.G. Lott's leaving, J.J. Walne took O. Vidler as partner. Thus up to the time of Thurmans acquiring the property an unbroken tradition of ironmongery ranging 113 years, and probably more had set an example to be followed.

In 1921 it was obvious that motor transport had come to stay and mobility was the key to the future. Accordingly a Model 'T' Ford van was purchased for delivery purposes and two motor-cycles with side-cars for the workshop. One was a 3.5 H.P. Sunbeam and the other a 3 H.P. Ariel. An ex-army Douglas was also purchased for Mr. Watts' supervisory work.

In 1924 the High West Street shop had a face-lift, a new double-fronted shop front with a central doorway and the floor of the front portion lowered to obviate the entrance steps. This curtailed headroom in the front cellar but as at that time it was only to be used for stores, bulk nails etc. and only by the staff, who quickly found out where the low skull-cracking beams were, it did not matter. The rest of the frontage was left alone.

It was now that the advantage of motor transport showed itself. The large and medium-sized country houses were cold, draughty and most of them dimly-lit with paraffin lamps or low-voltage electric plants. Moreover many were short of domestic water. The owners wanted more comfort and were willing and able to pay for it. Two teams for country work were arranged, one led by Fred Gillett whose ambition was beginning to be realized, and the other by Bert New, a very steady, reliable type who had joined Thurmans as an apprentice on his 14th birthday in 1908. Mr. G.W. Watts began to devote more of his time to workshop matters and supervising jobs in progress.

The electric grid system and piped mains water was still in the future, as was oil-firing and natural gas.

The work of heating country houses was not easy. Most had enormously thick inner walls and very many had important architectural features or portions of historical importance that must not be disturbed. Some of these houses had old heating systems already, mostly inefficient and in process of decay. The work of bringing these up-to-date was about equal to that of an entirely new installation.

Heating was by a large coal-fired furnace in the cellar, copper piping was prohibitive in price so all work was carried out in iron with innumerable and complicated fitments. There were not water impellers to force the water through the piping and radiators, and the circulation of hot water depended entirely on the skill employed in the 'run' and levels of the pipe work, to take advantage of natural forces, the difference in specific gravity of hot water leaving the boiler and the cool water returning.

One of the early houses to be 'heated' was Warmwell House, then occupied by Major 'Tommy' Foster. The difficulty there was a quantity of large blocks of stone embedded in the internal walls, usually just where one wished to lead a pipe from one room to the next. A hole 1.5" diameter on the entry side would become perhaps 2 feet wide on the other, to the removal of a stone block.

Another house presenting wall difficulties was Kingston Maurward owned by Mr. Cecil Hanbury, of 'Allen and Hanbury' fame, where the original outside walls were of brick, afterwards encased in Portland stone.

Athelhampton Hall, at that time occupied by Mr. Cochran was full of architectural features, particularly the hall and gallery that must not be disturbed.

The linen-fold panelling in the library at Chantmarle owned by Mr. St. John Hornby, caused much thought as no piping apart from the radiators must show and the panelling must not be moved. Modern small-bore easily-manipulated copper tube fed by an impeller would have saved many hours' work.

Melcombe Bingham, owned by Lady Grogan, was another job that needed great care to preserve the atmosphere of its centuries of occupation.

On the other hand, houses such as Moreton House (Cdr. Frampton), Clyffe House (Col. Kindersley), Kingston Russell (Mr. Gribble), presented no difficulties except heat loss through the great lengths of pipe involved.

In some cases stone flagged floors under which it was necessary to run 'return' piping could be awkward, as could the oak floorboards in upstairs rooms. These oak floors usually consisted of oak planks grooved on the edges, with iron strips inserted into the grooves, to hold the planks together and also to prevent under-floor draughts. Later buildings had tongued and grooved boards, all wood, and were simple to deal with.

17, South Street 1902
Mr Wake   Mr G.W. Watts   Mr Day   Mr W.R. Skyrme

17, South Street 1932

But the most infuriating delays were caused by the occasional uncovering of some unknown feature of archaeological importance, perhaps a built-up doorway or as in the case of Stour House, Stourpaine between Blandford and Shaftesbury, the discovery under a layer of plaster of large mural paintings on the walls of what was at that time the kitchen. Once the archaeologists were on the job they didn't want to leave.

Most of the larger country houses within a ten-mile radius of Dorchester were initially heated or renovated by Thurmans, and the installations serviced afterwards. In no case was an architect employed to draw up plans, the layout and whole installation being left to Thurmans.

Then it was the turn of the larger farmhouses.

Church hot-water heating although sometimes carried out, was not sought after because the results were never satisfactory. The very high roofs absorbed the heat as fast as the furnace could generate it, driving cold draughts from above down on to the congregation. The draughts were shocking and the furnace was rarely lit until Saturday night or early Sunday morning, then let out until the next weekend. The best that could be done was to ensure that one radiator was adjacent to the pulpit and another at the Squire's pew, and hope for the best.

Nevertheless many country churches were done but every effort was made to get permission to put in free-standing 'Tortoise' or similar stoves so that the congregation could at least see the heat even if they couldn't feel it.

Town heating jobs were if possible left to other local firms. The country houses occupied Thurmans resources and motor mobility was the key to success. Moreover these houses were capable of placing large orders for domestic goods and thus brought more business to the retail side of the business.

A ten-mile limit was aimed at, with a few exceptions, owing to the amount of daily travelling involved with somewhat uncertain vehicles.

During this period two 'bull-nose' Morris Cowley chassis were purchased and Mr. F.B. Legg, wagon builder of Long Bredy was given the job of making van bodies to suit. Mr. Legg being a good wheelwright, believed in strength with plenty of good solid elm and ash. The result was that although the bodies would have outlasted a dozen chassis, the weight was such that the poor little engines could hardly get going, empty, and when loaded with piping, tools, boilers etc. took considerable skill to arrive at their destination.

One van was used to supplement the growing delivery service, the other was handed over to Gillett's team, a three-wheeled Morgan acquired for Bert New's outfit and the two motor-cycle and sidecars scrapped.

There were of course no Trades Union rules and the men were allowed to put in what time they liked, often amounting up to 76 hours per week. There was also no rule about 'who does what'. The fitters cut their holes through walls and made good afterwards, took up floorboards and relaid them, and did simple brickwork when necessary: in fact they were a self-contained unit spurred on by the enthusiastic Gillett who found himself in his element at last. The thing was to get the job done with the minimum of inconvenience to the customer, and done so that there would be no failures or 'come-backs'.

The Trades Union movement was growing and several attempts were made to induce the workshop staff to join, but this matter was dealt with by the employees themselves and the management only heard about the visits of the officials after they had been shown the door.

Although motor cars were seen more frequently some still preferred their horses and carriage and would draw up at the front door and wait for an assistant to approach and learn their wants and wishes. Amongst the last of the carriage shoppers were Mr. Floyer of West Stafford and the Misses Williams, West Leaze, Charminster.

The two big days in the year's calendar were Candlemas Fair held on St. Valentine's day, February 14th, and Poundbury Fair on September 29th. Candlemas Fair has been well described by Thomas Hardy and others and it suffices to say that the stalls, booths and sideshows extended from the Town Pump both sides of Cornhill with a double row up the middle, and the overflow down High East Street to the Kings Arms, and both sides of High West Street to Holy Trinity Church and Godwins Corner[1]. Brandy snaps, toffee apples, sweets of all colours, cakes of all descriptions, fat ladies, a coal-black negro blowing fire from his mouth, another breaking carefully prepared and half-sawn-through chain around his biceps, fortune tellers and a dental booth for tooth extraction. At night naptha flares and paraffin lanterns and the pubs open 'til midnight. Good boisterous, and fairly honest fun. Marvellous days!

On the more sober side it was also the hiring fair at which farmers would engage carters, shepherds, general farm workers for the ensuing year. This procedure has also been written about and described by many.

A noted sale of bulls was conducted on this day in the Market, drawing buyers from all parts of England.

Poundbury Fair on September 29th was a business event; sheep, thousands and thousands of sheep, and some horses. There being no motorised transport, everything was brought in 'on the hoof'. It was possible to stand in High West Street in the early morning and see nothing but sheep as far as Greys Bridge, and beyond, just a huge mass of bobbing sheep's heads, each flock separated from the next by the shepherd, striding along almost up to his waist in sheep. And every other main road into Dorchester was the same, all wending their way to Poundbury. The noise of the sheep and excited dogs cannot be described, neither can the state of the roads and streets afterwards!

Thurmans always staged a small stall or stand (the only one there) on Poundbury, and as a result made many new friends.

At this time a self-generating gas plant called 'The Aerogen' was widely

---

[1] Now Horse with Red Umbrella

advertised and Thurmans were called upon to install several sets in houses out of reach of town gas supplies. Gas pipes were laid on to the various rooms and a 20-foot gantry erected in the garden outside, furnished with weights which on their gradual downward movement forced the fuel through a form of carburettor and in a gaseous form through the piping to the lighting points. Fuel used was high octane petrol called at that time 'Aviation fuel', and formed a very explosive mixture. These jobs were not looked forward to with delight. One of the first installations done was at Langmere Gate, Lyme Regis entailing over forty miles' travelling each day. 'Aerogen' plants gave satisfactory service but were at times temperamental, and soon gave way to the demand for private house electric plants.

Dorchester had its own Electric Light Company, the generating station being in Church Street, now a residential area. But this of course could only cater for the town itself and nothing outside, and at times was a little uncertain. The twin engines were large and if their own starting gear (compressed air) failed, manpower could not turn the huge flywheels so an urgent message sent to Thurmans to borrow a small portable farm engine, Petter or Lister, together with a fitter to get the big fellows going again before the storage batteries ran out and Dorchester reverted to oil lamps and candles.

The benefits of electric lighting were quickly realized by country dwellers and resulted in a wave of demands for sets generating at 110 volts or 50 volts and in a few cases even 25 volts. None of these could carry current consuming appliances, only lighting. The wiring of the houses and buildings was a simple job compared with central heating work. Electricity would run either uphill or down at pleasure and the cables were small and unobtrusive. The major part of the work was the layout of the powerhouse, usually a shed or small building close to the main house, the installation of a generating engine on a concrete base, the engine being either Crossley, Blackstone, Campbell or Lister, the dynamo usually a Crompton, and the storage batteries.

A few 'automatic' plants were installed. These had very small storage cells of only sufficient capacity to start the engine, and the current was fed to the lighting points direct from the set. They were only suitable for small jobs and there were several disadvantages. The engine had to be kept in tip-top starting condition otherwise the stored current in the small batteries would be exhausted; if more than one light was switched on the engine would start up resulting in a fluctuating light and the noise of the engine exhaust in quiet surroundings at night was disturbing. However, they were comparatively inexpensive.

The servicing and maintenance of these plants and of others originally installed by other firms outside our normal territory made the ten-mile limit quite inoperative and was a step towards a much wider field of operation.

Proper water supplies to country houses and farms were demanded. Wells with bucket and windlass were usually already in use where there were no suitable springs. It was Thurmans job to install pumps, piping, manual gear or engine, either a Petter, Lister or Hamworthy. If the low water-level in the well was 30 feet or under below the surface of the well-head, the pump was situated immediately over the well; if over 30 feet the pump was placed on a platform down the well, in some cases 100 feet down. This work carried high insurance rates but fortunately no claims had to be made. In addition roof storage tanks usually had to be installed or renewed, in the house, stables and farm buildings. The fitters on these works were usually Bert New who joined the firm as an apprentice in 1908 and 'Hammer' Gill who joined in 1913, who was the possessor of enormous biceps and had a habit of exclaiming if a rusted joint or bolt gave trouble, 'Gi'e'or 'thick 'ammer.'

A rather more sophisticated system of water supply was the 'Hydram' utilizing the 'Hydraulic Kick' of a running stream to raise water from the feed stream. It could also be made to obtain its power from a stream and raise water from a more pure supply from a nearby spring.

Once installed it cost practically nothing to run, the only wearing part being a rubber diaphragm to be renewed every three or four years.

Many of these Hydrams were installed. One at Cheselbourne for Mr. Bennett raised water from river level to the top of the Down, feeding by gravity two or three farms.

Another installed at Clover Leaf Farm, Portesham, at the expense of Mr. Mansfield Hardy supplied most of the inhabitants of Portesham and was the first piped water supply to a village in this area. In cases such as these the farmer would excavate trenches for pipe work, and fill in afterwards when the piping had been laid and tested.

An unusual pumping engine which had to be serviced was a hot air engine installed at East Hill House, Charminster. Power was produced by hot air rising from a furnace built into the lower part of the apparatus and pressing against a piston of some 3.5 feet to 4 feet in diameter which in turn was geared to the water pump. The whole affair was huge, inefficient and dependent on large supplies of wood and coal fuel and labour. It did the job of raising water from a shallow well in the scullery to a tank in the roof, but quite naturally had limited appeal and was the only specimen in Thurmans orbit.

Still on the subject of water supplies, this being a hard water district there was a steady sale for water softeners, principally the Permutit, to private households and hand laundries. The installation of these was a simple job and the owner saw to the periodic infusion of fresh salt.

Bill Dean having been killed in the war, the mantle of leadership of the young generation was assumed by a lad named Fall who carried on the tradition of practical jokes but in a rather less robust manner. One escapade caused Charles Street to be blocked to traffic. They had somehow obtained a stuffed parrot and perched it on the roof gutter overlooking the street. It was spotted in no time at all and a crowd collected, all trying to entice someone's pet down. It was only after a blithe spirit had shinned up the rainwater pipe, which collapsed under the strain, that the hoax was exposed.

In high summer the tinsmiths workshop being directly over the forge and under a low roof, became unbearably hot. It was the custom to send two lads armed with a bucket of whitewash and a spray syringe on to the roof to cool it. The whitewash deflected a little of the heat. The Rector of St. Peter's the Reverent Metcalf, a cleric much respected but with a solemn mien and always in full clerical dress, chanced to be walking up Charles Street while the de-heating process was in progress. The first intimation the management had of the affair was the appearance at the office door of a figure, incoherent with rage, clad in some sort of black and white costume. A quick investigation revealed the fact that on a hot and airless day, a sudden wind had sprung up just as his Reverence was passing and had blown the contents of the spray in his direction. Strangely, no-one else seemed to have noticed the 'sudden strong wind'. This escapade cost the management a new wide-brimmed clerical hat, the price of cleaning a frock-coat and trousers and possibly a front seat in the next world.

Rev. Metcalf

Although workshop outside activities are dealt with at some length bench work and smithing was continued, repairs to all sorts of utensils, and tools, lawnmower grinding, the making-up of sheet-metal ware and sheep horn brands. The Dorset Horn Breeders Society issued registered numbers to members' flocks and in order to retain control authorized Thurmans to be the sole makers of these special brands. The original brand submitted to the Society for approval is on view in the Dorset County Museum.

In 1926 Mr. W.R. Skyrme died after a two-days' illness and his son J.E. Skyrme had to take on the responsibility of the business with the backing of a loyal, enthusiastic and capable staff, headed by Mr. G.W. Watts.

In 1928 the Bath and West of England Agricultural Show returned to Dorchester and was held on the Exhibition Field, Slyers Lane at the top of Stinsford Hill. Thurmans took an island site, erected a roofed and floored wooden stand, divided the stand into twelve separate compartments, each furnished with a different phase of ironmongery, persuaded manufacturers to loan demonstrations of their various commodities to supplement local staff and also special exhibition pieces. One such piece was a 'Whirlwind' vacuum cleaner, perfect in every detail and mounted on a halfpenny. It was kept busy every day picking up french chalk on a miniature carpet. As the two shops had to be kept going as well and there was of course a big influx of visitors into the town the strain on the staff was heavy and the stand and shops were crowded with sightseers and customers for each of the four days.

The show was visited by the Prince of Wales (afterwards King Edward VIII) who was kind enough to pass some complimentary remarks about Thurmans displays.

At this time, factory mass-produced goods were gradually replacing many handmade sheetmetal goods but the demand for register plates, stove-piping and soot doors for the increasingly popular type of free-standing portable kitchen ranges increased, as did the popularity of the special quick-boiling kettle. A reputation for making 'specials' to the customers' individual requirements also helped to keep the sheetmetal section as busy as ever.

An example of one 'special' arose from the decision of Messrs. Bedford and Jesty, the producers of 'Silver Springs' watercress at Bere Regis, to expand their output to the North of England. Under the direction of Mr. Fred Jesty a sheet zinc replica of the Bere Regis beds was made complete with running water for an exhibition at Leeds.

A fresh consignment of watercress was sent up each day and it is understood that the presentation started a very strong and lasting business connection for 'Silver Springs.' It will be realized that the standard of 'live' exhibits in the 1920's had not reached the sophisticated levels attained today and this was somewhat of an innovation.

In 1922 wireless was in its infancy, for the normal household a crystal and cat's-whisker affair with earphones, but there were a number of local enthusiasts and it was decided to stock the necessary parts required. The sales were excellent but the project was dropped after a few years owing to these customers' spending half their spare time discussing circuits, their successes and their failures. The loss of sales time made the project uneconomic.

For the same reason the sale of bee-keepers' appliances had been dropped some years previously.

In 1922 a firm of Sheffield cutlers, Herbert Robinson & Co. were approached

Nat Seal Lambs Foot Knife

to produce a 'Lambs Foot' pocket knife of a design that was traditional, had been in use by shepherds for a great number of years, possibly centuries and that should be exclusive to Thurmans. It was decided to commemorate the name of Nat Seal, a colourful character who had been one of the last of the West Country long-distance sheep drovers and about whom many tales were told. Nat had been a customer for his knives in the very early days of the business. A stencil was made from an old photograph and etched on the blades. These knives were sold in quantities until the 1950's, when Herbert Robinson's was the subject of a 'take-over' and it became impossible to obtain a satisfactory quality under the new mass-production methods.

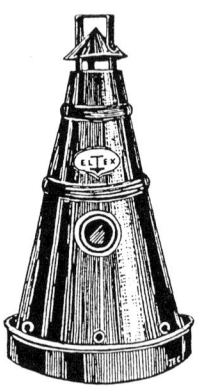

Greenhouse heater

Chapter 3 1930 - 1939

Up to the 1914-18 war the retail (front shop) staff brought their packed dinner sandwiches on market days and retired to one of the stock rooms, in relays, to consume them. During the war they were allowed to go home for their dinner as a slight relaxation, and closing time was brought forward to 6 p.m. These conditions were adhered-to until the second world war when closing time was brought forward to 5 p.m. and opening time 8.30 a.m. After 1945 closing time settled at 5.30 p.m.

An old custom universally kept up until 1939 was the erection of boards six or seven inches wide, painted matt black, put up one in front of each display window as a mark of respect and mourning on the day of the funeral of a member of the staff, or of a near relative of one of the staff, or of a prominent citizen.

By 1931 it was obvious that the South Street shop was not only not adequate for the number of customers and for the display of the variety of new goods coming on to the market, but it was impossible to make provision for the future 'walk-around' and open display systems that were already appearing in the cities. Also the building was old, had been altered, internally, time and time again and some parts were positively unsafe. So the decision was taken to demolish the whole site with the exception of the old workshops at the rear and rebuild as a walk-around, open floor, two-storey shop. Reinforced concrete buildings were appearing in the larger towns but none so far in Dorchester, nor in fact in Dorset. This required planning by someone with experience and Messrs. Jackson & Greening of Bournemouth who had recently erected the new bus station in Bournemouth, were asked to draw up plans. The tender of Messrs. Watts Bros. of Pound Lane, Fordington, by now in the hands of the sons of the two brothers who had done the 1905 alterations, was accepted and a competent clerk-of-the-work engaged. The work was done in three sections starting at the rear, was commenced at the end of 1931 and completed early in 1932. During the work business carried on, not quite as usual but apparently to the satisfaction of customers, who flocked in, many obviously out of pure curiosity. The High West Street shop benefited by the custom of those who found the builders' noise and dust disturbing. Lighting, heating and plumbing was of course done by Thurmans own staff and the heating was effected by an oil-fired furnace, an innovation at that time for Dorchester. This attracted several orders for similar apparatus. A tribute must be paid to Messrs. Watts Bros. and the clerk-of-the-works who between them completed the job on time, and ensured that no after-snags developed.

Although the new open-floor idea of shopping was accepted by the townspeople at once, the village and farming circles did no take to it readily. It

1938 Transport

H.A. Harvey   R. Toop   J.W. Dibben   O. Bley   J.E. Skyrme   F.W. Gillett   H.G. New   B. Hammett

was soon realized that the smell was at the root of the trouble. New paint everywhere, too clean, too tidy and it didn't smell like a proper ironmonger's shop. So sundry little rearrangements of displays etc. were made and shallow baths of creosote and balls of tarred twine were hidden under display stands and counters. That put the matter right.

Just prior to this rebuilding the workshop staff, forge and machinery was moved from its original home at the rear of the South Street shop to the stables, coach-house and a small building at the rear of the High West Street premises, access being both from High West Street and Colliton Street. At the same time the old Rectory was attended-to. New roof timbers, walls strengthened and the original earth floor cemented. Enough original tiles were saved to cover one half of the roof and the rest were obtained to match, as near as possible. The front door stone archway was in danger so it was removed block by block, to be built into the wall of the new South Street building as being the safest place available and also available for viewing by the public.

The period 1932-1939 was a time of expansion. By 1938 the transport had increased to four vans, five various cars and one motor-cycle. Two vans were for workshop use, one for delivery in town and the nearer villages, and one for a regular weekly delivery service to all villages, farms etc. up to about a fifteen-mile radius including Bridport, Weymouth, Portland, Wareham, Sherborne and Blandford. The workshop vans were able occasionally to help out by dropping goods off on their way to country jobs. The various cars were for travelling representatives, small urgent deliveries and supervisory work.

Advertising was speeded-up. Regular advertisements had been displayed in the *Dorset County Chronicle* and later in the *Dorset Daily Echo* for many years, also hand-out leaflets etc. and an occasional fully-illustrated catalogue, the *Hearth and Home* issue amounting to 152 pages and the *Farm and Field* to 80 pages. An innovation was the *Monthly Bulletin* a 30-page illustrated catalogue, produced each month, contents according to the season, and posted to 1,500 selected customers. The person in charge of all this was Miss Eve Stone. As a girl she acted as assistant to her father, a coastguard stationed at Camborne, Cornwall. On his retirement in 1915 he came to live in Dorchester. Miss Stone joined Thurmans as a typist, graduated to and built up the publicity section and died in 1957 still in harness.

Publicity included an expanding programme of stands at Agricultural Shows. The Dorchester Show displays tended to become more comprehensive, and a refreshment tent was added, in which tea, sandwiches, cakes and snacks were provided for customers both actual and prospective. This facility was run by the staff ladies under the charge of Mrs. Rabson, normally a sales assistant. No alcoholic refreshment was offered; there was plenty to be had on the Corn Merchants' stands, and Eldridge Pope's beer tents. Thurmans 'rest tent' proved very popular, offering the chance to 'put one's legs up for a few minutes' accompanied by a cup of tea out of a proper teapot. It was noted that a goodly number of hardened old Show-goers normally associated with one long trek around the beer tents, came and expressed pleasure at the arrangements. These old sinners generally managed to raid the floral decorations for a flower for the button-hole! But never mind, they left orders behind them for delivery next week.

Display stands were staged at Melplash Show each year and Gillingham and Shaftesbury Shows. These two last were aimed at Blackmoor Vale customers. Melplash Show wore a garden-party atmosphere, was thoroughly enjoyable and strengthened Thurmans connections in West Dorset areas contacting people who normally would have been drawn to Bridport or Axminster.

Yeovil Agricultural Show, for a one-day event, was a big one. A display was mounted for three years but was then dropped as it was found the bulk of orders resulting were for destinations North of Yeovil, uneconomical from the delivery angle. It will be realized that at that time delivery had to be free; the practice of charging for delivery was still in the future and would have been bitterly resented.

In 1936 the Royal Counties Show visited Chickerell and was notable as being the only one that was not favoured by fine weather. It rained solidly for some days before and one day during. The show-ground being on yellow clay became a quagmire. Many ladies removed shoes and stockings and paddled around in bare feet, a practice not usual in those days. Packing-cases were broken up and laid as duck-boards on and around the stand and had disappeared into the mud by teatime, to be followed by a fresh layer the next morning. There must have been at least five layers of boards to be subsequently ploughed up by the owner of the ground. Nevertheless the public were very good-humoured, seemed rather to enjoy it and spent freely.

It was impossible accurately to gauge the result of these Shows. An instance can be quoted of a lady who came into the shop demanding a certain type of lawn-mower that she had 'seen at the Show' on Thurmans stand. It was explained that that model had been out of date for the last couple of seasons and was no longer manufactured.

However, she pursued the point and brought along a leaflet that she had been given 'at the Show'. The leaflet was dated some four Shows ago. Many orders arrived from different parts of England, sometimes months afterwards.

Besides these outdoor activities stands were taken at various Trade Exhibitions at Dorchester Town Hall, the Women's Institute at Top o' Town[1], the Sidney Hall at Weymouth[2], and in conjunction with Messrs. Shepherd & Hedger (furniture) and Ney's (fashions and mannequin parades) at the Hotel Burden, Weymouth[3].

Manufacturers were most co-operative in lending the services of their own trained demonstrators for any special sales drive and also lending out-of-the-ordinary exhibits and cut-away working machinery, much to the pleasure of scores of small boys.

During the 1930's two particularly important agencies were accepted. A

[1] Now Buzz Inn
[2] Now Asda Car Park
[3] Now Prince Regent

franchise for the whole of Dorset for bottled gas (Calor), then in its infancy, and for heat storage cookers (Esse).

These two products quickly got going, giving the retail section the opportunity to sell Calor appliances, cookers, heaters and lighting, and the workshop the work of fixing them. A fitter was sent to the factory for training and very soon a second fitter had to be allocated to Calor also. Installations, cookers and lighting being the chief items, were carried out throughout the county and the work of distributing refills of gas became so heavy that dumps were established at West Lulworth, Bowleaze Cove, Chickerell and Portesham. Installation required great care but was relatively simple, the only outstanding really difficult installation being lighting Woodsford Castle, then tenanted by Mrs. Stephens.

The Esse agency took considerable sales drive by the retail staff to get it underway as the Aga, a heat storage cooker imported from Scandinavia had been on the market for some twelve months already and had established a reputation. But the Esse was a better job, being more elastic in operation, providing a warm kitchen, and being more robust. The first installations were at Bridport, Lyme Regis, Corfe Castle, Swanage, Blandford, Sherborne, Hawkchurch, Gillingham and Sturminster Newton and especially in hotels and boarding-houses in Weymouth and proved very successful. These, together with a few large and spectacular installations such as the Royal Naval Hospital, Portland, Portwey Hospital, Weymouth, Portland Dockland, Borstal Institution at Portland, Bovington Camp etc. made a great impact. Sales snowballed until there was not an area that did not have its quota of coloured pins on the progress map. Two experienced fitters were allocated for this work and found the installations and servicing to be full-time job. At intervals one or two more fitters had to be switched from normal work to assist. The team was under the leadership of Bert New.

An Esse Cooker

Thurmans Horticultural Show 1938
combined with celebration of Mr Harry King's 50th year at Thurmans

The Staff and their families

R. Hodinott W. Mayo J.W. Dibben F.W. Gillett W.Keats A.C. Treasure W.C.Watts A. Hansford O. Bley
F. Bubier L. Templeman H. New H.S. Foden E.A. Wheadon - Hinton

Miss E. Watts Mrs Hancock — Mrs Wheadon — Mayo, Jnr R. Hancock W.Hopkins R. Trevett
A.J. Ellery - Short K. Hoddinott F. Gosney A. Gill — Mrs A. Smith Miss A. Read Miss G. Collins

Mrs Gosney Mrs New Mrs Hoddinott Mrs Mayo Mrs Harvey H. Harvey G.W. Watts H. King J.E. Skyrme
Mrs M.L.L. Skyrme (with baby Elizabeth) Mrs E.M. Skyrme Miss E. Stone Miss Walker
Mrs Gillett — Miss J. Collins

Hoddinott Jnr. Ellery Jnr. Two children Treasure Jnr. Miss Hopkins Jnr. Miss Gill Jnr. Two children
Mrs Hopkins Mrs Treasure Mrs Gill — Mrs Trevett

Activities were supposed to be confined to Dorset as Hampshire was in the care of Scott & Scott of Bournemouth and Devon was looked after by Whipple Bros. & Rowe of Exeter. Somerset and Wiltshire were not very well covered and consequently installations were carried out for Mr. Ashworth Hope, the organ music composer at Marston Magna for instance, and the Hon. Mrs. P. Pleydell-Bouverie, Landford Gate, Salisbury and some more around Warminster: Maiden Bradley; Willsford, Marlborough; in Wiltshire, around Crewkerne, Yeovil and Chard in Somerset and by arrangement with Whipple Bros. & Rowe, Axminster in Devon.

The normal area covered was, however, bounded on the South by Lyme Regis, Portland, Tyneham and Swanage. On the East by Upton, Poole, Wimborne and Chettle, on the North by Shaftesbury and Sherborne and on the West by Misterton and Uplyme.

An important by-product was orders for new kitchen utensils and equipment as each kitchen was brought up-to-date.

During this period 687 installations of Esse cookers were carried out.

A workshop job worthy of mention was for Mr. Leonard Sturdy of Trigon, Wareham. The Trigon water supply was drawn direct from the heath land and although being pure and palatable was strongly acid, attacking iron whether galvanized or not and quickly making it porous. It was decided that stainless steel, then established but only just out of its infancy, would have to be used. Accordingly the whole system was carried out in that metal. Piping, fittings, hot water cylinder, tanks in the roof and even the taps. Much had to be specially fabricated. The work was very expensive and subject to many delays but in the end proved more economical than constant renewal of iron.

An evening Cricket Team was formed and played local and village teams such as Frampton, Cheselbourne and Martinstown. Thurmans seldom won a match but thoroughly enjoyed themselves. The match of the year, however, was the 'Inter-Shop' competition between the two branches for a silver cup. Rivalry was terrific, and honours fairly well divided.

In 1933 a Horticultural Society was formed, the very able secretary and mainspring being W. Hopkins (Hoppy). For the Annual Show in August a marquee was set up on the lawn of the proprietor's house, 'Duffryn,' Herringston Road and classes for exhibits to suit everyone arranged: vegetables and fruit for the men, flowers, flower-arranging and cake-making for the ladies, wild flowers for the children. the judges were usually Mr. Dight of Rew, Mr. Lunn of Martinstown, Mr. Goodchild the head gardener at Ilsington House and for the cakes, Mr. Humphries of the Spinning Wheel Restaurant, Dorchester[1]. Substantial prizes were offered, largely provided by interested manufacturers.

The employees averaged 43 in number so together with wives, and children under 10 years of age an attendance of 70 to 80 was catered for. Under the MC.

---

[1] now Woolwich Building Society

'Ammer Gill, simple sports, skittle alley, sack and potato races, walking the plank, and for the men a race from Duffryn, up Manor Road to the Grammar School and back via South Court Avenue, filled the afternoon together with a close, detailed and critical inspection of each others' exhibits in the marquee. A sit-down tea on the lawn followed and after that a 'mystery tour' for all by coach. This gave an opportunity for the travelling staff to air their knowledge of the countryside and houses passed, to the indoor employees. Then back to Duffryn for coffee and a stand-up snack, and that was the end of a day of enjoyment for all and jolly hard work for a few.

The 1938 Society show was a double event, incorporating not only the usual proceedings, but also the 50th anniversary of Harry King's entry into Thurmans, and his presentation.

In May 1936 Mr. G.W. Watts completed his fiftieth year with Thurmans and was the guest of honour at a Presentation Party held at 'Duffryn.' This gave an opportunity of expressing the very high regard for him, by the seniors right down to the smallest office-boy. In fact everyone present wanted to say a few words and the goodwill expressed was most touching. The little anecdotes passed around were numerous, based on so many years of working together, and in some cases most illuminating to the management.

In 1936 Messrs. Dibben Bros. the last of the trio of established ironmongers so active at the turn of the century, closed down owing to the death of Mr. A. Dibben, one of the partners, and his son Mr. J.W. Dibben joined Thurmans as a travelling salesman.

Days that were looked forward to were the visits of Bostock and Wombell's or Sanger's Circus. On the afternoon of their arrival a Grand Parade was conducted around the town - elephants, camels, mounted cowboys, Red Indians, all looking extremely warlike, piebald horses with plumes and buxom fairies perched on top, clowns and of course the band. These circus days drew most of the countryside into Dorchester, and themselves brought a considerable amount of business. for the larger animals the move to the next town was 'on the hoof' by road and many were the stories told of locals rounding a corner and being confronted by a string of angry camels.

'German Bands', a party of quite accomplished musicians, playing martial and popular tunes on brass, as they paraded through the streets with collecting-boxes had disappeared, to be followed for a while by similar groups, but not so accomplished, of ex-service and disabled men.

The 'Hurdy-Gurdies' or barrel organs with a little monkey perched on the top had also gone, much to the relief of many people. A little of that was pleasant enough, but to have one anchored for half an hour outside the shop door was more than enough.

The retail side had been having its rapid changes of merchandise. Aluminium in quantity had become available in 1920, displacing cast-iron and copper in the kitchens, and now it was the turn of stainless-steel, desirable but highly expensive.

The medical profession was of great help to the ironmongery trade. Periodic discoveries that enamelled ware, especially the continental supplies imported in great quantities, contained soluble lead salts in the glaze meant the scrapping of the old and purchase of new, and in time aluminium came under fire owing to harmful salts forming when used with certain foods, the people resorted to enamel ware again.

Electrical appliances assumed importance and complexity, and bathroom furnishings became the vogue. The output of new ideas and gadgets made it increasingly difficult for the department buyer to sort out worthwhile and reliable goods from the dross. Farming methods were changing, milking machines became very important, and all milk and dairy appliances, but the real change-over to mechanized and electrical farming was still in the future. In 1933 the Milk Marketing Board had been formed and in a dairy area such as this had a profound effect, although the agricultural community were rather slow to take advantage. With the increased output of liquid milk the continued shortage of help, farmhouse cheese-making commenced to decline, and disappeared almost entirely later. Tractors being now universal meant a change-over from horse-gear to larger stocks of machinery tools and although Thurmans did not deal in tractors or their repairs, repairs to ancillary equipment broken by perhaps unskilled tractor drivers certainly did. The growth of gardening by townspeople resulted in a separate gardening division being formed and it was fortunate that so many of the staff were keen and knowledgeable gardeners themselves.

1938, and it seemed as though war with A. Hitler, Esq., was going to be unavoidable. The third war in Thurman's history, but this time it was going to be a 'soldiers war'; everyone was going to be in it. Business life carried on as usual but with an undercurrent of uncertainty, and vague plans for carrying on if the worst happened, beginning to crystallize.

The beginning of 1939 brought the certainty of trouble and endless conjectures. Should a small stockpile of C.R.C.A.[1] iron sheets be accumulated, what about barbed wire, would supplies of Calor gas for those dependent on it for cooking be available, what about anthracite for Esse Cookers, what staff would be left? What? When? How? Which? One thing was certain, the authorities were well ahead with plans for regulations, controls, rationing, permits etc. covering every field. The officials were coming into their own.

The older and obviously unfit staff joined a voluntary spare-time service of their choice. Workshop and drivers joined the A.F.S (Auxiliary Fire Service) and enjoyed the excitement of the fire engine, others as Wardens, Ambulance Service drivers, Special Constables etc. Females joined St. John's Ambulance Brigade, the Red Cross or A.R.P. first-aid units. The Observer Corps and L.D.V. (Local Defence Volunteers) seemed to be the only ones left out.

On the outbreak of war the 'call-up' routine went into action and younger staff disappeared in rotation. It was impossible to replace them and female assistants

[1] cold rolled cold annealed

1938 A portion of the machine shop - Workshops at rear of 64 High West Street.

were engaged and proved a great success. Although quite untrained, they were keen to learn and soon were able to handle all the less technical matters. Blackout was a nuisance; both shops were surrounded by glass with many roof lights and all had to be close-covered.

The 8 o'clock curfew, a custom hundreds of years old, was of course stopped, as were all church bells.

At the beginning, panic buying and hoarding by the public was rife and it took much diplomacy to curb some of this and leave a fair share for others.

The country delivery vans were commandeered at once by the Army and one was spotted in France with the name 'Thurmans' still decipherable. The workshop vans, being older and rather tatty were left.

The ironmongery trade was in a better position than some. Agriculture was essential to the nation, supplementary petrol was allowed for servicing farming matters, and supplies of iron, steel, and some manufactured metal goods were available on permit. But oh! the endless form-filling and arguments with the various Ministries, and the improvisations that had to be made to keep customers, farms and households just ticking over.

By 1937 (two years before the outbreak of war) the workshop at High West Street was bursting its seams and there was no room for additional machinery. A portion of the garden being some 3.5 feet higher than the floor level of existing building and yard was excavated and a steel frame building erected. The side framing was composed of girders which not only carried a corrugated iron roof but also cross girders for the support of overhead cranes and lifting gear and overhead shafting. This work was carried out by Thurmans staff. During excavations a Roman roadway was uncovered, complete and unspoiled; even the rust marks and grooves made by Roman vehicles were plain to see. This attracted the attention of the Museum Archaeologists who were considerably more delighted with the find than Thurmans were with the delay.

An iron plate was let into the workshop wall below the level of the garden surface and opposite the roadway which of course continued on its way undisturbed. This enabled the section of road with its foundations, aggregate, camber and surface to be examined in the future if desired.

The enlarged workshops, 40 per cent greater floor space than before, proved its value during the war when outside and distance work had to be curtailed and a period of repairs and 'make do and mend' was necessary. Customers' appliances, machinery, tools, which normally would have been scrapped as worn-out were patched-up to last 'for the duration'. Bench work had come into its own.

A serious blow that Thurmans had to suffer was the death in October 1939 of Mr. G.W. Watts, still in harness after 54 years as manager, and still as alert, forward-looking and active as ever. The loss of his personality and advice was keenly felt.

Chapter 4 1940 - 1949

The war had put very considerable strain on the staff left, after the withdrawal of those eligible for the Services and as the shortage of supplies gradually became worse it became difficult to staff and stock two large shops. Consequently it was with relief that in 1942 the Ministry of Food requisitioned the front portion of the High West Street shop for use as a British Restaurant, leaving the workshops and stores and yard at the rear in Thurmans occupation. This arrangement was much to the satisfaction of the tenants upstairs, the two middle-aged daughters of Mr. G.W. Watts, who soon got used to the aroma of fish and chips rising through the floorboards, and much appreciated the extra warmth.

It is not the purpose of these notes to record the impact of the war on the town in general, only to say with thankfulness that Dorchester did not suffer the devastation endured by many of its neighbours, Sherborne, Yeovil, Portland, Chapelhay.

At long last it was over and staff drifted back as released from the Services. All who applied were re-instated but three or four had found fresh interests further afield or had married girls in another part of the country and decided to seek fortune in that county. One who did not come back was Mr. Leslie Templeman who decided to join his father and grandfather in their saddlery business in Cornhill, Dorchester. Although saddlery as such has been given up, the business flourishes.

1939 had marked a definite end to an era and to a 'way of life.' Change was in the air and it seemed as though much of the joy and fun of business would be missing. There always is change, evolution is bound to occur, usually for the better, but a quotation from a report to Parliament much later, on January 15th, 1962 by a committee headed by Sir Gilbert Upcott and Sir Colin Anderson reads: 'The quality of life and the convenience and pleasure of living are being steadily eroded.' And that process was in being during the post-war years.

1945 brought an end to the war but it did not bring peace to the ironmonger. Rationing, controls, permits, supply certificates, and form-filling went on as usual, but now the public who had shown such wonderful spirit during the fighting were weary and tired of 'make do and mend' and were impatient to get their affairs going again. The retailer being the last link in the supply chain was the easiest to 'have a go at'. Dividing fairly between customers the meagre supplies coming in, and combating the greedy ones was a very real worry. Fortunately, in a small town strangers were spotted fairly easily by some member of staff, and overtures by those on the prowl, even amounting to bribery and willingness to pay 'over the odds' were quickly frustrated.

The agricultural community were the most difficult to deal with. Food production had been and still was of vital importance. The farmers had had, quite deservedly, a rewarding time and had in their pockets money which they could not spend. Farm machinery and tools were rundown and worn out and were hard to come by. Form-filling and paper-work added zest to lamentations. Vermin, pigeons, etc. had increased during the war, what about cartridges to save the nation's food supply? Cartridges came along under permit in dribs and drabs and were doled out a box of 25 at a time. Many were the dodges to obtain more, a visit twice a week in the hope of 25 each time; the man getting his quota and his wife following-up for more, a little later. Yet who could blame them; everything was topsy-turvy.

Supplies of goods were erratic; the designs especially of domestic items were pre-war, but the quality of much was poor. During the war one got used to makeshift and substitute materials but now someone in manufacturing circles was cashing-in on shortages and the willingness of the public to accept shoddy goods and workmanship.

The supply of raw metals was difficult. Cast-iron and steel were still on very strict permit. Copper and brass, difficult, but aluminium especially sheeting, fairly freely available. The trouble with aluminium was that each consignment seemed to vary in its alloy content, making welding and fabrication tricky.

An obscure manufacturer of refrigerators, named Power Master and based at Hamworthy, Dorset, was able to obtain endless supplies of aluminium sheets and electric motors. Moreover, the refrigerators although of a comparatively unknown make were good, with standard and high-class components. A contract was arranged. Thurmans salesmen got busy, delighted to have something to sell that was not swamped by restrictions, and it was not long before the farmhouses got their first taste of better times, their refrigerators.

The fleet of vehicles was built up again. Wartime stresses having been too much for the old vans, a Land Rover was added and proved to be quite invaluable; an additional van was necessary and a light trailer to be attached to any of the ordinary cars.

Any war brings forth a flood of new materials and new inventions. Because of vital urgency, ideas that would be uneconomic to develop by the ordinary manufacturer in peace time were given full rein and costs did not come into the picture.

One of the first revolutionary ideas to come forward was plastics. Hailed at first with derision and suspicion, and quite rightly so, as owing to the anxiety of various small manufacturers to climb on the band-wagon, the wrong type of plastic was often used for the wrong job with a quick failure to follow. As yet no indication of the innovations they were to contribute, and the metals they would displace was evident. It was impossible at that stage to imagine the dairymen using a plastic bucket instead of the solid old tinplate with iron handle, or mucking-out his cow-yard with a plastic broom, but they were accepted and after a while become the natural and normal thing. With the winning-over of the countryman the Plastics Age was on!

Fresh agencies were sought and as Esse cookers had opened up the prospect of better kitchens, Bendix Rotary Washers and Dishmaster washing-up machines seemed an obvious choice and territories for sales and service were arranged. Both were good machines and made satisfied customers. Kitchen cabinets, enamelled sink units and free-standing cupboards all in the then-popular cream and green colours followed but as these latter items were not mechanical and required practically no fixing or servicing there was plenty of competition from builders' merchants who were expanding.

Another innovation which proved to be very successful was the sale of coal, both household and boiler fuel in bags. This tied-in nicely with Calor gas for delivery purposes. Stocks were held in both 28 lbs and 56 lbs bags.

Garden Fork

Chapter 5 1950 - 1966

The High West Street premises were de-requisitioned in September 1950 and as the supply and staff problems were still difficult the front portion was let to Mr. A.M. Willats, an antique furniture dealer until 1957.

In the early 1950's factory production potential, built-up in wartime had to be used, resulting in a flood of goods of all types appearing, some of it unfortunately ill-conceived, good to look at but not practical in use. The department buyer's job became critical but as some of the most respected names in manufacturing circles were occasionally guilty it was not always possible to sift the wheat from the chaff. Instances cropped up of hot-water cylinders and tanks being made up of metal two gauges thinner than normal, closed-top tanks imperfectly galvanized on the inside seams so that they quickly rusted through. A range of most attractive chromium-plated aluminium teapots was offered and taken up and eagerly bought by customers. They came back again within a week, minus spouts. The welding of spouts to the teapot bodies was insecure. One can imagine the chaos caused at the tea-table by such a happening.

One cause of all this bother was the great increase in newsprint and glossy magazines, the coloured advertisements proving irresistible to a public starved of attractive possessions for so long.

Another cause showed itself in connection with a heating boiler, nationally known through massive advertising. A series of these boilers were installed and a proportion, not a small proportion, leaked water as soon as normal pressure was turned on and the fire lit. Replacements were sent and many of these also leaked. Things became so bad that in answer to strong representations a senior from the factory arrived and after examining a row of 'faulties,' said, "Well, it's like this, old man, we can only return a certain proportion of faulty bodies to our foundry each week, or we'd have a strike on our hands. The rest have to be sent out and chance whether they're all right or not!"

Thurmans extra expense in having to take out the first and install a replacement were reimbursed but nothing could replace the delays, inconvenience and mess endured by the customer.

The decline of the cattle market was a blow to Dorchester. Much of the selling was done through Ministry arrangements and Sturminster Newton seized the opportunity to build a large, up-to-date market and built up a very large connection for calves.

Poundbury Fair finished as such and became a sheep sale, of importance nevertheless, held in the Weymouth Avenue fair field.

Candlemas Fair had died out and the only sign of stalls in the streets was the 'barrow boys', fruit and vegetables.

Wednesday gradually ceased to be the most important day of the week and as the country people were getting motor cars they tended to spread their shopping and business jaunts over the days until Tuesdays and Fridays, previously fairly quiet, rivalled Wednesdays in the crowded streets.

In 1946 Thurmans followed the current trend and formed itself into a private limited company, all shares being held by the Skyrme family. The original directors were J.E. Skyrme and his brother-in-law, O. Bley.

Whether this was a wise move or not is open to discussion. It was current and correct business practice at the time and it certainly spread responsibility, ensured that top authority was always present on the premises and perhaps gave a little added status when dealing with suppliers. On the other hand it certainly made a lot more unproductive office work, and was a deterrent to giving snap 'off the cuff' decisions that are so often necessary in a small or medium-sized business.

Poker

It had been hoped to re-start pre-war staff social activities, cricket and the staff flower and vegetable shows at Duffryn. Cricket had to be abandoned. The older members were six years older, were tired and disinclined to run up and down a cricket pitch and the young ones had their motor-bikes. The flower show had also to be shelved. Catering problems, the necessity of still squeezing the maximum food out of gardens and allotments, and not wasting half of it in trying to grow show specimens, the wanderlust of the young members and the death of the mainspring secretary, W. Hopkins (Hoppy) in February 1949, prevented its resumption.

Instead, every opportunity was taken to celebrate any happenings, by organized visits to Boscombe Hippodrome, the Regent and the Pavilion at Bournemouth, preceded by a tea or dinner as the case may be.

A memorable gathering was the celebration dinner of H.G. New's 50th year of service with Thurmans on 24th February 1958 at the Antelope Hotel, Dorchester, at which staff and wives totalled 75 persons, and Bert New was presented with a television set.

Another gathering was at a dinner followed by a play at the Pavilion, Bournemouth on March 10th 1955 to celebrate the 80th birthday of Mrs. E.M. Skyrme, the widow of Mr W.R. Skyrme who had died in 1926. Mrs. E.M. Skyrme died in 1958 in her 84th year, keenly interested in every aspect of the business and everyone in it, to the last.

Many, in fact most employees had their own transport and were beginning to take their fortnight's holiday further afield, as an extra day was allowed which, if they had begged a few extra hours off on the previous Saturday, gave them three weekends away.

An attempt was made to change Thursday half-day closing to all-day closing every Monday, thus making a five-day week for all, but as Genges the drapers[1] were the only shop willing to do the same, and the rest were fiercely against a change, the project was dropped.

In 1957 Mr. A.M. Willatt's lease terminated and the High West Street shop was re-opened as an Agricultural Branch with special reference to the expanding dairy market, milking machines and all dairy supplies. Mr. Arthur Smith who had shown a very keen interest in all farm matters while acting as outside representative, was put in charge, helped by Mr. Reg. Hoddinott, a trainee named Kevin Fox, a porter-cum-handyman H. Trevett and Miss Elizabeth Skyrme, daughter of J.E. Skyrme, who had joined Thurmans in 1956 after her initial training with Coopers of Oxford and who was intensely interested in farm matters. She studied for and in 1957 sat for the Intermediate Examination of the National Institute of Hardware, obtaining the N.I.H. second prize, the Pond prize for the highest marks in the written portion of the exams., and was one of the only four throughout Britain to obtain a distinction. In 1959 she also sat for the Final and was elected to Associate Membership of the Institute, being the first girl ever to have been so admitted. She was also Secretary of the Dorchester and District Young Farmers' Club until retiring under their age-limit rule, and was four years Secretary of the Wessex Branch of the National Federation of Ironmongers.

[1] on corner opposite The Horse with the Red Umbrella

At Arthur Smith's request he was soon allowed to get out 'on to the road' which was his real interest, with special instructions to concentrate on agricultural matters. Miss Elizabeth was then made manager of the branch.

In 1960, William, son of J.E. Skyrme, having received his training with Malletts Ltd., ironmongers and builders' merchants of Truro, entered Thurmans business but preferring a wider field, resigned after a while and took a position in Malaya, and subsequently with oil companies in Nigeria, Houston U.S.A. and Brazil.

Mr. O. Bley died in 1950 and Mr. Joe Dibben was made co-director.

Appearances at Agricultural Shows were resumed as soon as the Agricultural Societies got going again, more or less on the same lines as before but with a very different selection of articles on display.

In 1951 the Bath and West of England visited Dorchester again. This time the ground selected was on Maiden Castle Farm off Weymouth Avenue. Thurmans of course took a large space, dividing it into sections each with manufacturers' demonstrators implementing the local staff. By now many of the post-war new productions were fairly readily available and were now reliable: Bendix washers, Coldrator refrigerating equipment, Clifford rotary cultivators, Allen scythes, stainless steel tools and of course, Esse cookers.

It rained for three days up to the afternoon prior to the show's opening, and the ground was a quagmire. Then the sun shone. Being on chalk, the surface dried overnight forming a springy carpet over the mud below. Three glorious sunny and hot days followed.

1951 Dorchester Agricultural Show Stand

As a matter of fact in all the years of staging extremely vulnerable open stands on exposed show grounds and exhibiting a mass of easily-spoiled ironmongery, only three wet days were endured, one at Gillingham, one at Melplash and one at Weymouth during the Royal Counties Show in 1936.

Up to the early 1920's 'Commercial Travellers' or 'Manufacturers' Representatives' as they preferred to be called travelled by train with a large quantity of enormous cases filled with samples of all the goods their firms made. They booked rooms at the Antelope Hotel or the King's Arms for two or three days and produced perhaps three or four cases per day for the retailers' inspection. These men were of good standing, representing substantial suppliers, very knowledgeable and truthful and willing to discuss trends and what their firms were likely to produce next year. Their advice was valued and their visits were an education. At a later stage the larger suppliers would hire a 'stock room' at the hotel, lay out their samples and invite their local customers and those from neighbouring towns to come and inspect. This practice saved a lot of time for everybody.

With the increase of motor traffic came a great increase in the number of 'commercial' calling, and a rapid decrease in quality of the callers. Eventually most of them became a positive nuisance, especially as so many carried the same line of goods, and many knew little about their job. This obtained chiefly among those representing wholesalers or 'factors'. The upsurge of wholesalers could be put down to the advent of the Purchase Tax system by which almost anybody could register as a wholesaler, obtain preferential terms from a manufacturer and while holding a very minimum of stock himself, have orders dispatched to his trade customers direct from Works, thus throwing his work, expenses of holding stocks and risks on to the manufacturer. In fact this added an extra link to the chain of distribution and increased costs. The advantage of the system seemed to be that it made it easier to collect the tax. However, all had to be seen by the retail buyer just in case something different was pulled out of the bag.

Another menace was the innovation of the female traveller who was inclined to gain audience where her male contemporary feared to tread. Common courtesy demanded the buyer's attention until the lady had finished talking. The Buyer lived a hard life.

Of the making of books there is no end, and much study is a weariness of the flesh

Whoever thought that one up was most certainly an ironmonger. So far the office, the hub and nerve-centre of any business has hardly been mentioned, except as the vehicle by which H. Harvey was promoted from packing room to sales section, and Miss Stone who joined the staff in 1915 and progressed through the main office to found her own department of publicity. Another of note is Miss Squibb, a country girl who, while in the Land Army during the second world war fell into a threshing machine drum, had her right arm amputated, took typing lessons immediately on leaving hospital, and applied for a job, was taken on as a typist and at the time of writing is still holding the position with quiet, unobtrusive efficiency.

Others who must be mentioned are the Daubeney sisters of Parsonage Farm, Fordington. Gillian Daubeney was engaged as secretary-typist. When she left to get married, the younger sister, Edna, took over the job. When Edna left to get married another sister, Rita, stepped into the position. When Rita left to get married, Mr. Daubeney was appealed to, but the supply of daughters had now run out. They were a good lot of girls and very efficient. Commercial office work requires a special type of intelligence denied to those whose instinct is to get out and about and meet the customers face-to-face on their own ground. It was the job of the management to hold the scales between the clash of personalities. The office quite rightly held that a sale was not concluded until the bill was paid and the money in the bank. This, however, was cold comfort to a salesman, proud of his day's work and expecting congratulations. In a country district where a large proportion of customers are farmers or in some way to do with the land, the usual accountancy methods of getting bills paid and the books kept 'straight' just wouldn't do. It is difficult to get a tidy-minded office manager to understand that a farmer's income doesn't come along neatly in an envelope each week, but that at times his money is in the ground waiting to sprout, and at other the harvest has been reaped and sold, be it corn, wool, Easter lambs or fat cattle. Of course a farmer should have sufficient capital at disposal to smooth out these fluctuations which are seasonal, but in practice it doesn't work out that way.

A point that sometimes caused confrontation between strict accountancy and the Buyer's department was the question of slow-moving stock. The view taken by management was that holding a comprehensive stock of odds and ends the customer wanted or might want, fostered goodwill and saved a customer's drifting around and possibly leaving Thurmans altogether. This probably old-fashioned view, in the management's opinion overruled the question of a certain 'line' paying its own shelf rent. But of course it upset the sales-to-stock-turn ratio at the end of the year, and the accountant's dream of quick stock-turn and a high ratio of nett profit.

DIRECTORS J. E. SKYRME. J. W. DIBBEN.   TELEPHONE 700/1

THURMANS OF DORCHESTER LTD.

IRONMONGERS

Farm, Dairy & Garden Branch	17 SOUTH STREET	*Workshops*
64 HIGH WEST STREET	DORCHESTER	4A COLLITON STREET
Telephone 1686	DORSET	Telephone 700 (Ex. 1 & 2)

In the early days of the business it was the custom to send out bills quarterly and expect to have them paid yearly, the retailer in fact acting as unpaid banker.

It was fortunate indeed that the manufacturers also took a lenient view and seemed content to have their accounts cleared when the traveller next came around with the new range of samples. This state of affairs persisted until the early 1900's. Ledgers, journals, day-books were fixed-leaf books with all entries handwritten, until the end of the first world war then loose-leaf ledgers, massive affairs with genuine pigskin covers were introduced, made by Kalamazoo Ltd. As business expanded these ledgers proved to be too unwieldy, and a set of smaller loose-leaf books, the 'Moors Modern Methods' were substituted. These were in use up to the end of this story and probably are still used in the 1970's. Card indexes were used for stock control, mailing lists, etc. The first telephone was on the Bell Telephone Company's system and number was 6XY2. When the Post Office took over telephones the number was 70 and when business demanded extra lines, 700/1/2. Office machinery was kept to all the usuals, plus an addressing machine, a pre-paid envelope system, an automatic answering telephone switched on after the usual business hours, and a postal franking machine. Cash registers were installed at each of the departments at the High West Street shop and a central cash desk in charge of Miss A. Read at South Street. A cash desk was decided upon as it relieved pressure on the salesman at busy times and also provided another pair of eyes to note any irregular happenings at the open display stands. Shop-lifting was very occasionally encountered but it is believed that it was of a very minor category until the surge of petty crime in the 1950's.

The office gradually grew in importance although paperwork was kept to a minimum but each time Whitehall had time to think up something fresh the complexity and expense mounted. The advent of Milk Factories and later the Milk Marketing Board led to a better management of the farm dairies, farmers became more businesslike and the monthly milk cheque helped the credit position. It is a true saying that 'what is made in the field can be lost in the office' but thanks to a very reliable and interested staff, bad debts were very infrequent in every case only for small amounts.

'A day during which nothing is learned is a day wasted'. This was the motto drummed into the staff, young and old, constantly.

It is the duty of the ironmongery trade to accept and train youngsters, usually sons of other ironmongers who intend to carry on the tradition of work and service to the public. Afterwards some branched out and started their own business. Some of Thurmans trainees founded very successful businesses in Winchester, Monmouth, Banbury (Hartwells who have branches throughout the South Midlands), Newton Abbot, and one joined Woolworths and became their general manager in the Bahamas, while still in his early thirties. Several of the staff asked for sons to come for initial training and they all eventually made good in the wider world.

Although 'training' is usually associated with apprentices and junior staff, it was necessary to ensure that seniors were kept up-to-date and to that end three-day visits to the British Industries Fair at Birmingham were arranged each year, Mr. Skyrme taking with him a couple of seniors each time in turn, Mr. H.J. Fry the

> **THURMANS of DORCHESTER LTD.** IRONMONGERS
> 64 HIGH WEST STREET . DORCHESTER . DORSET   Telephone Dorchester 700/1
>
> Directors:
> J. E. SKYRME
> D. M. M. HARRIS
> E. M. SKYRME

senior buyer, Mr. Hancock an assistant buyer, Mr. W.H. Hopkins manager at that time (the 1930's) of the High West Street shop, Mr. E.A. Wheadon, workshop manager, etc. Visits on similar lines were arranged for the Ideal Homes Exhibition in London and to any important agricultural shows within reasonable distance.

Mr. J.E. Skyrme being a Fellow of the National Institute of Hardware had the duty of attending the annual five-day Residential Trade School at Abingdon. These courses were of the utmost value, not only in keeping up-to-date and being aware of future trends explained by the lecturers, but also in making and retaining contacts with fellow-ironmongers from all over Britain and also manufacturers who supported the movement.

Usually senior staff were taken too, in rotation, Mr. H.J. Fry, Mr. J.W. Dibben, Mr. W. Johns and of course Miss Elizabeth who, being the only girl student, managed to combine a little of the social side with the weight of constant lectures and practical exercises. Some of the lectures were given by qualified outside professional lecturers, others by the Fellows of the Institute. One subject chosen by J.E. Skyrme was a paper on 'Buying to Sell.'

Being Vice-Chairman of the Wessex Branch of the National Federation of Ironmongers, followed by the office of Chairmanship carried the obligation of attending monthly meetings in London and the annual four-days conference. These were held in rotation at Eastbourne, Scarborough, Sandbanks, Folkestone, Newquay, Bournemouth, London, Torquay, Brighton and Harrogate. The conferences were far from the popular conception of a grand orgy but although wives were present and a certain amount of social events arranged, the committee saw to it that the maximum amount of business was on the agenda and in the meantime informal chats between delegates from all over Britain were especially valuable.

The Wessex Branch held its own monthly meetings at which trade matters were freely discussed. An educational talk by a manufacturer or by a public body, for instance the Ministry of Employment, or the Police on Security, or by Customs and Excise on some new regulations, or by a member who would give a paper on some aspect of business, or a new idea that he had tried out.

A rather controversial talk was presented by J.E. Skyrme on 'A Hardware Store Without A Stockroom', an explanation as to how a business in Dorchester

1957 64 High West Street Shop

1963 Corner of China Cellar. 64 High WestStreet

with only unattractive bulk supplies, cement, bagged coal, barbed wire, in stockrooms out of customers' vision, was managed. This system was subsequently installed by several other ironmongers with success.

It so happened that when one of the Wessex Branch meetings was held in Dorchester, the popular chairman that year was H. Jeffery of Axminster, who had claimed to be some connection of the Red Judge. Accordingly, unknown to Jeffery, the Oak Room at the Antelope Hotel was booked for the evening and the chairman's table decorated with fetters, manacles, leg and body-irons, handcuffs, etc., borrowed from Dorset County Museum. It is recorded that this was the most orderly meeting yet held, the chairman only having to hold up a length of Bridport rope for background noise to subside.

The Branch also formed a Bulk Buying Group, by which members pooled their requirements of standard lines to be delivered to one address and from there distributed to the members. This enabled these bulked goods to be obtained at very competitive prices.

These Branch meetings were held at a different town each time, ranging through East Devon, Somerset, Dorset and South Wilts.

Membership of the Electrical Contractors Association and the Coal Utilisation Council also helped to broaden one's outlook but make considerable demands on one's spare time.

In 1962 the need was felt for accountancy to be represented on the board and Mr. D.M. Harris who had been chief clerk and company secretary for some time joined the board.

In January 1965 Miss Elizabeth Skyrme was elected as junior director because of her specialized knowledge of agricultural matters, ability to bring a younger approach to meetings and to give more 'family' representation.

By 1962 it was obvious that in the cities and larger towns the pattern of High Street trading was rapidly changing, that the quick-turnover, quick-profit shops, supermarkets, ladies' dress and shoe shops, cut-price and cut-value shops were going to take over the popular sites and that business offering slow-moving and durable goods would have to find other accommodation in less important areas. Accordingly plans were made and in 1963 work commenced and was completed to make the High West Street shop suitable for the whole of the retail business, leaving the workshops at the rear as they were already.

Mr. John Stark, architect, was asked to prepare plans for submission to the Planning Authority, and Messrs. George Cake & Co. were engaged to carry out the alterations. The usefulness of the long iron and tube store equipped when the business was run in conjunction with the foundry, with massive cast-iron racks to store bar, channel and round iron bars, and general castings, was in the past. So the racking was removed, the floor levelled and the place done up as an up-to-date showroom. This joined up with the front shop and gave a continuous showroom 190 feet long. The cellars, one large one about 90 feet long, and two smaller cellars connected to it were excavated to full depth to give extra headroom and fitted out as a new china and glass department, one of the smaller cellars for kitchenware and the smallest into a trade museum. As speedy communication was considered essential, telephone extensions were carried to each sales point. A small matter with unforeseen consequences was the introduction of 'ramps'. Owing to differences of floor levels, two shallow steps ran right across the front portion of the shop with another two steps down to the level of the new long showroom. As a convenience for those with invalid chairs or perambulators, a sloping ramp was made beside these steps. it was soon found that not only were the ramps being used for these purposes but found that strong, able-bodied customers were using them too in preference to the two shallow steps. In fact, at times a little queue formed to use them.

The 1922 frontal alterations had been carried out largely to do away with the short flight of steps from pavement to the original shop but it was not realized until now what a deterrent to business steps could be. Another use was found for the ramps, too. It took little time for the junior visitors to discover that the ramps were splendid things for wearing out the seats of trousers while mum was selecting her purchases.

The whole job was completed in good time in an excellent manner under the direction of Messrs. Cakes foreman Mr. George O'Brian, Thurmans workshop staff co-operated with the plumbing and lighting requirements and no snags or comebacks were experienced.

A tribute must be paid here to Mrs. M.L.L. Skyrme (wife of J.E. Skyrme) who entered this story in 1932 and not only helped with encouragement and advice on every fresh venture but organized day and evening demonstrations of practical cooking, both on the Esse cooker which was permanently under fire in the South Street showroom, and also on her own Esse cooker at home. She instigated the china and glass department in the renovated cellar at High West Street, acted as buyer for that department and trained Mrs. Shuttleworth, a sales assistant, to be in charge of the sales of china and glass.

The 17 South Street premises were sold to Allied Food Suppliers, the 'Home and Colonial Stores', and the stock and staff moved to 64 High West Street in June 1963.

The business then became a self-contained unit, and much easier to control, and the customers remained loyal and followed.

Towards the end of that year a portion of the outside display space was purchased by the Ministry of Transport to form a run-in for a bus stop. This still left room for a worthwhile outside display of goods, allowed vehicles bringing or fetching goods from Thurmans to pull in away from the traffic stream, and gave passengers waiting for their bus an opportunity to study the window display.

It was to be expected that the list of customers included some notable people. The Max Gate household were often in the shop. Thomas Hardy paid infrequent visits, leaving most household affairs firstly to Emma Hardy and afterwards to Florence. When he was personally involved he had little to say. His first wife, Emma, had one remarkable trait which caused much trouble to Mr. Watts, the manager. She had a new dress nearly every year and her bicycle had to be painted the new colour to match. If the reader has ever tried to match a piece of material the shading of which varies according to the angle of the light striking it, with a coat of paint which doesn't, he will understand what Harry King the paint-mixer had to put up with.

Mr. Herman Lee, Thomas Hardy's great friend was interested in the prospect of producing oil in the Portesham district and was frequently in the shop, purchasing tools and bits and pieces.

Lawrence of Arabia, known then as Aircraftsman Shaw, was often in the High West Street shop, which he preferred, riding his Brough Superior motorcycle from Clouds Hill. It so happened that J.E Skyrme also had a Brough Superior at that time and these two appeared to be the only ones in the County. So naturally the visit ended with a long discussion on the merits and performance of Brough Superiors. On the occasion of Lawrence's last visit he bought two birch garden besoms and needing them urgently, tied them on to the motorcycle, the handles along the petrol tank and the broom ends on the saddle. Watching him going down High East Street perched on the top of the lot, it seemed that he would take off at any moment with a black cat, for a voyage over the moon.

Three days later he was killed on the Bovington road and his beloved machine smashed to pieces.

Llewelyn Powys was a fairly frequent visitor and always made a splendid entry, clad in a black cloak with wide-brimmed black hat and followed by two or three attendant ladies. A chair was quickly produced and once enthroned, Powys made known his wants and wishes.

The two Misses Gordon, relatives (said to be sisters) of General Gordon of Khartoum were charming people, gentle in approach, in speech, liked by everybody, and very appreciative of any little service done for them.

During the period of Maiden Castle excavations in 1934 Sir Mortimer Wheeler liked to select the tools and supplies for his assistant excavators, and knew exactly what was wanted.

The Rev. E.A. Milne of Cattistock, the hunting parson, and more recently Ralph Wightman of broadcasting fame were frequent callers and brought with them the very aura and spirit of Dorset, the former usually in hunting kit on his way to or from the meet.

Of those well-known in industrial circles, one calls to mind Mr. Angus Hambro (Hambro's Bank) of Milton Abbey; Mr. Vesty (Shipping and Union Cold Storage) at Kingston Russell; The Hon. Mrs. Harmsworth (Press) for some time at Athelhampton Hall; and also the Ali Khan who spent much time there; Mr. Field (shipping, Holts' Lines) of Longthornes and Mr. St. John Hornsby (W.H. Smith & Sons, booksellers) of Chantmarle.

On June 30th, 1966 the Skyrme family sold the whole of their share holdings in Thurmans to Messrs. Davis & Hadley, Electricians and thus severed a family ownership of sixty-eight years.

At that date the Roll of Honour of service with Thurmans included; H.G. New, 53 years of service; A. Gill, 53 years; F. Bubier, 50 years; F.W. Gillett, 52 years; L.F. Turner, 51 years; J.E. Skyrme, 46 years; R.E.J. Hoddinott, 46 years; A.J. Ellery, 43 years; E.A. Wheadon, 36 years; and four more of 20 years and over.

Of those who had died while still at Thurmans were; G.W. Watts, 54 years; H. King, 53 years and H.A. Harvey, 35 years. Also Miss Stone, 42 years.

At a party given at 'Duffryn' in November 1963 for and in honour of these old employees, presentations were made and a great number of reminiscences, some now incorporated in this story, were exchanged.

THE DORSET GENERAL HARDWARE STORES

Mr Gollop, Charminster Dorchester 1896

Bought of W. H. C. THURMAN,
WHOLESALE AND RETAIL
GENERAL & FURNISHING IRONMONGER
ENGLISH & AMERICAN TOOL DEALER, OIL, COLOUR, & IRON MERCHANT.
MANUFACTURER, BELLHANGER, GASFITTER. REPAIRS IN ALL BRANCHES.
RANGES, STOVES, & GRATES.   IMPLEMENTS & DAIRY UTENSILS.

Date	Item	£ s d
July 1	6 lbs of Steel Rose Nails	– 1 3
Aug 25	2 gns of Linseed Oil	– 4 6
	1/2 of White Lead 1/6 14 lb of gnd Ven Red 1/6/9	1 0 3
	28 lb of Putty 1/6 7 lb of gnd Oak Oke 4/	– 8 6
	66 lb of Steel Rose Nails asstd	– 9 0
	1 lb of Wool Clouts	– 2 3
	3 gross of Screws assorted	– 3 4
	2 lb of Lamp Black 1/ 1/2 lb of Chinese Red 8	– 1 3
Nov 18	bottle of Bench Polish	– – 6
	7 lb of 1½" Clout Nails	– 2 4
	7 lb of Plough Bolts assorted	– 3 6
	1 gross of Washers 8 7 lb of Pat Rose Nl 1/3	– 1 11
	7 lb of Wire Nails 1/- 1 bottle of Stain 1/-	– 2 0
	14 lb of Pat Rose 7/6 1 Hanging Lamp 4/9	– 7 3
21	2 Plane Irons 1/3 2 lb of galvd Nails 10	– 2 5½
Dec 1	3 prs of Short Bed Handles	– 1 2
	2 – Chest "	– – 8
	1 Saw 6/9 Sash Cord 1/-	– 7 9
	Hammer 1/8 Gimlets 2/5	– 4 1
	½ doz Brad Awls	– – 10
	1 Bit each 1/2, 1/0, 2/3	– 5 3
	6 doz Screws	– 1 9
	2 gross of Screws	– 2 8
	10 lb of C.S. Clout Nails	– 2 11
	14 lb of gnd Ven Red	– 3 6
	3 prs of 14" T Hinges	– 1 9
	7 lb of Pat Dryers	– 2 0
	7 lb of Wire Nails	– 1 5
	Carried Forwd £	5 7 0½

		£ s d
	Brought Forwd	£ 5 7 0½
	1 Dinner Knife	– 1 0
	2 Kegs	– 2 6
Dec 2	12 lb of Dumans Solder	– 1 6
	3 Files 1/3 1 Oil Can 6	– 1 9
7	1 – 18" Shell Auger	– 1 6
	1 – 1½" Jennings Bit	– 1 2
	3 Drop Escutcheons	– – 9
24	7 lb of 2L Pat Rose Nl	– 1 3
		£ 5 18 5½
		5 5
2 Jy 6/97 Recd 7/5/-	£	5 13 0

W. H. Thurman

1973

It seems that perhaps undue emphasis is placed on workshop matters. The retail section though the major part of the business and most in the public eye, could with trained and efficient staff allowed to use their own initiative, run along with the minimum of supervision. Much of the varied stock in trade can be seen in the photographs and portfolio of catalogues and leaflets issued.

On the other hand much of the workshop activities, in fact nearly every work job presented its own problems and was therefore much more interesting.

Although the story is of one ironmonger in one small town, a history on similar lines could be recorded of a great number of others, in other towns, having the good fortune to keep their identity in spite of urban crawl.

It is the privilege of the elderly to regard days that are gone through rose-tinted glasses. But what a wonderful way to spend a life! And what good fortune to have lived at a moment in time when computers and property developers were still specks on the horizon. Long hours of work, yes, each one crowded with problems and queries, that made Sundays and Thursday afternoons all the more enjoyable. And what a splendid team to work with, their lives and the lives of their families bound up with one's own.

And now in 1973 conditions and trends are changing again, or perhaps have never stopped changing. In the absence of a crystal ball it is not possible to do anything but guess at the future but it seems that possibly the High Street supermarkets and multiples will have to do some thinking. For some years American tendencies have been to establish shopping centres some miles outside the cities where parking space for thousands of cars can be allowed, the centres themselves providing under-cover shopping for practically everything a human family may need or can be persuaded to buy, and in fact provides a 'day-out' for the family and no parking problems. The movement is gaining momentum in this country. So far the nearest centre to Dorchester is on the outskirts of Bournemouth. Parking no problem, branches of two Banks and a Post Office, no scrambling on pavements and no sense of being pushed around. Another has recently been opened this side of Exeter. In the Midlands with greater concentration of people there are plenty, and it has recently been announced that Littlewoods, already for some years in the walk-around store business, are entering out-of-town shopping centre projects. Will the establishment of shoppers' precincts, started in rebuilt Coventry, in operation to a limited extent in Weymouth, proposed for South Street Dorchester, provide an answer, or will the growth of two cars per family and the well-known aversion of car drivers to walking 200 yards away from the car, especially when carrying a week's supply or parcels, kill High Street precincts except where unlimited parking can be provided in a very central position? The writer is very happy to leave that problem on someone else's desk.

J.E.S.